INTRO

Semiotics

Paul Cobley and Litza Jansz

Edited by Richard Appignanesi

TOTEM BOOKS

First published in the United States in 1997 by Totem Books
Inquiries to PO Box 223, Canal Street Station
New York, NY 10013

Reprinted 1998

Distributed to the trade in the United States
by National Book Network Inc.,
4720 Boston Way, Lanham, Maryland 20706

ISBN 1 874166 55 2

Library of Congress Catalog Card Number: 96-061951

Printed and bound in Great Britain by
Biddles Ltd., Guildford and King's Lynn

If you go to the right cocktail parties, or hang around the foyers of the right cinemas, or read the right Sunday colour supplements, or watch the right late night arts programmes on TV, then you will know that "semiotics" is a valuable buzzword.

The Pre-History of Semiotics

Early precursors of semiotics include **Plato** (c. 428-348 BCE*) whose *Cratylus* ponders the origin of language; and **Aristotle** (384-322 BCE) who considers nouns in his *Poetics* and *On Interpretation.*

The word "semiotics" comes from the Greek root, *seme,* as in *semeiotikos,* an interpreter of signs. Semiotics as a discipline is simply the analysis of signs or the study of the functioning of sign systems.

The idea that sign systems are of great consequence is easy enough to grasp; yet the recognition of the need to study sign systems is very much a modern phenomenon.

IT SEEMS TO ME THAT THERE IS A DIFFERENCE BETWEEN THE CRIES OF ANIMALS AND THE SPEECH OF HUMANS. IT IS THE DIFFERENCE BETWEEN **NATURAL** SIGNS AND **CONVENTIONAL** SIGNS.

prrr

*BCE - Before the Common Era

4

One of the most notable debates on signs in the Ancient world took place between the Stoics and the Epicureans (around 300 BCE in Athens).

The crux of the matter concerned the difference between "natural signs" (freely occurring throughout nature) and "conventional" signs (those designed precisely for the purpose of communication).

For the Stoics especially, the quintessential sign was what we know as the medical symptom.

The symptom remained the model sign for the Classical era.

The major foundation for the Western interrogation of signs was laid in the Middle Ages with the teachings of **St. Augustine** (354-430).

Augustine developed his theory of *signa data* - conventional signs. Contrary to Classical commentators, he promoted such signs as the proper objects of philosophical scrutiny.

GOD.

GOD. I WONDER WHAT MADE ME SAY THAT?

He also served to narrow the focus of sign study by pronouncing on the way in which words seem to be the correlates of "mental words".

Augustine's narrowing of the focus was to have a serious impact on subsequent sign study.

Other scholars, such as the English Franciscan, **William of Ockham** (c. 1285-1349) exacerbated this version of the sign.

THE MAIN CATEGORIZATION OF SIGNS CONCERNS THOSE THAT ARE MENTAL AND PRIVATE, AND THOSE THAT ARE SPOKEN/WRITTEN IN ORDER TO BE MADE PUBLIC.

This, in turn, underpinned the work of **John Locke** (1632-1704) in his *Essay Concerning Human Understanding* (1690).

I SAW IN THE EXAMINATION OF SIGNIFYING PROCESSES A BASIS FOR A NEW LOGIC.

Although these figures in European philosophy are in some senses proto-semioticians, it is not until the 20th century that a full-blown semiotic awareness appears, under the auspices of two founding fathers.

7

Ferdinand de Saussure (1857-1913)

Saussure was born into an academic Geneva family in 1857.

At the age of 19 he went to study languages at the University of Leipzig where he was to publish, two years later, a famous paper on the "Primitive System of Vowels in Indo-European Languages".

Following completion of his thesis, Saussure left for the École Pratique des Hautes Études in Paris where he was to teach Sanskrit, Gothic and Old High German.

AT THIS STAGE I WAS MORE INTERESTED IN SPECIFIC LANGUAGES IN HISTORY RATHER THAN A GENERAL LINGUISTICS.

Here he stayed for ten years before being enticed back to Geneva to teach Sanskrit and historical linguistics.

In 1906 the University of Geneva, by fluke, provided the catalyst for him to produce a landmark in linguistics and, subsequently, semiotics.

Saussure was assigned the task of teaching a course in general linguistics (1906-11), a task he had not previously undertaken, and dealing with a topic upon which he would not publish in his lifetime.

Nevertheless, when Saussure died in 1913, his students and colleagues thought the course was so innovative that they reassembled it from their preserved notes and published it in 1916 as the *Cours de linguistique générale*.

In opposition to a "historical" - **diachronic** - linguistics which looks at the changes which take place over time in specific languages, Saussure pursued a **synchronic** linguistics. He presented an analysis of the state of language in general, an understanding of the conditions for existence of *any* language.

The *Cours* focussed on the nature of the linguistic sign, and Saussure made a number of crucial points which are integral to any understanding of the European study of sign systems.

Saussure defined the linguistic sign as a two-sided entity, a **dyad**. One side of the sign was what he called the **signifier**. A signifier is the thoroughly material aspect of a sign: if one feels one's vocal cords when speaking, it is clear that sounds are made from vibrations (which are undoubtedly material in nature). Saussure described the verbal signifier as a "sound image".

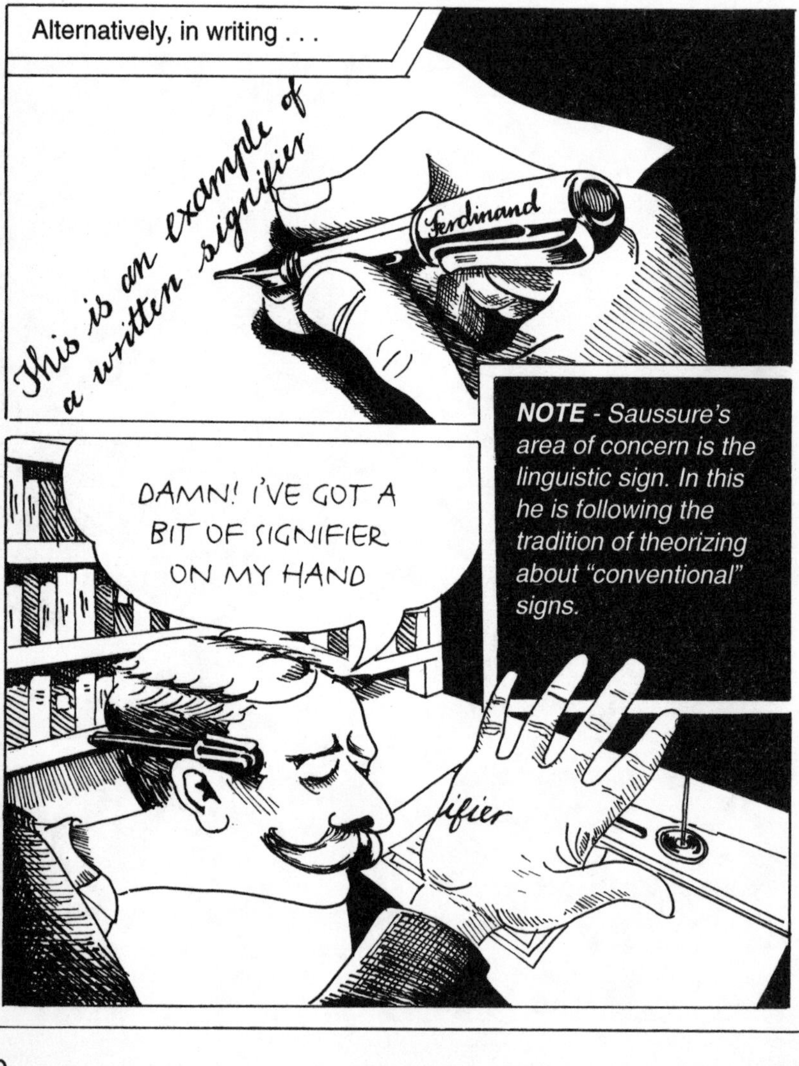
Alternatively, in writing . . .
This is an example of a written signifier
Ferdinand
DAMN! I'VE GOT A BIT OF SIGNIFIER ON MY HAND
ifier
NOTE - Saussure's area of concern is the linguistic sign. In this he is following the tradition of theorizing about "conventional" signs.

Inseparable from the signifier in any sign - and, indeed, engendered by the signifier - is what Saussure calls the **signified.**

This is a **mental concept.**

If we take the word "dog" in English (made up of the signifiers /d/, /o/ and /g/), what is engendered for the hearer is not the "real" dog but a mental concept of "dogness":

CANINE, QUADRUPED, BARKS, HAS SHARP TEETH, WAGGLY TAIL, BURIES BONES, EATS BISCUITS, HOWLS, FETCHES STICKS, GROWLS, URINATES ON LAMP-POSTS

The "real" dog might be a Great Dane, West Highland terrier, a spaniel, a lurcher, a wolfhound etc. rather than a general dog.

THE CONCEPT IS GIVEN PRIMACY IN SAUSSURE'S SCHEMA

The inseparability of the signified (mental concept) and the signifier (material aspect) leads Saussure to offer the following diagram:

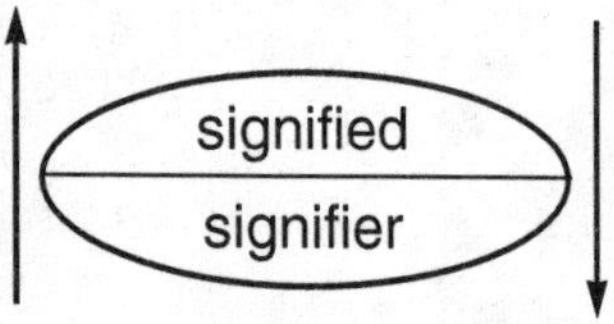

signified
―――――――――
signifier

Clearly, Saussure believes that the process of communication through language involves the transfer of the contents of minds:

The signs which make up the **code** of the circuit between the two individuals "unlock" the contents of the brain of each.

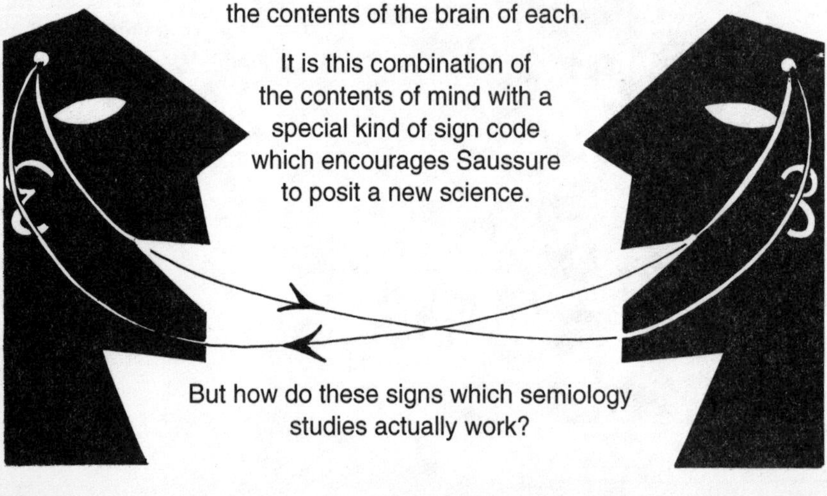

It is this combination of the contents of mind with a special kind of sign code which encourages Saussure to posit a new science.

But how do these signs which semiology studies actually work?

Central to Saussure's understanding of the linguistic sign is the **arbitrary nature** of the bond between signifier and signified.

The mental concept of a dog need not necessarily be engendered by the signifier which consists of the sounds /d/, /o/ and /g/. In fact, for French people the concept is provoked by the signifier *"chien"*, while for Germans, the signifier *"hund"* does the same job.

For English speakers, the signifier "dog" could, if enough people agreed to it, be replaced by "woofer", or even "blongo" or "glak".

That is to say, there is no natural reason why the signifier "dog" should engender the signified. The connection between the two is arbitrary.

A SCIENCE THAT STUDIES THE LIFE OF SIGNS WITHIN SOCIETY IS CONCEIVABLE; IT WOULD BE A PART OF SOCIAL PSYCHOLOGY AND CONSEQUENTLY OF GENERAL PSYCHOLOGY; I SHALL CALL IT SEMIOLOGY.

Saussure uses the term *semiology* as opposed to *semiotics*. The former word will become associated with the European school of sign study, while the latter will be primarily associated with American theorists.
Later, "semiotics" will be used as the general designation for the analysis of sign systems.

The only reason that the signifier does entail the signified is because there is a **conventional relationship** at play.

Agreed rules govern the relationship (and these are in action in any speech community).
But if the sign does not contain a "natural" relationship which signifies, then how is it that signs function?

For Saussure, the sign signifies by virtue of its **difference** from other signs. And it is this difference which gives rise to the possibility of a speech community.

Note: This principle of difference that gives rise to a system should be remembered when we go on to consider post-structuralism.

He describes the way in which the general phenomenon of language (in French, *langage*) is made up of two factors:

parole - individual acts of speech

langue - a system of differences between signs

Langue can be thought of as a communal cupboard, housing all the possible different signs which might be pulled out and utilized in the construction of an instance of *parole*.

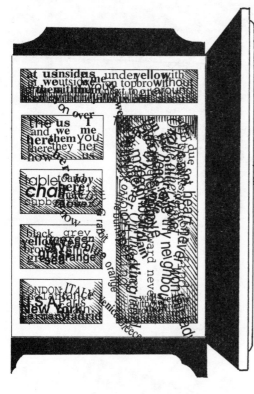

Clearly, the fact that language is a system (*langue*) used by all, means that it is also a social phenomenon through and through.

But note also that the system is **abstract** - like a successful game of chess, there is rarely the need to stop and consult a rule-book to check if a move (or an utterance) is legitimate. The rules are known without necessarily needing to be continually tangible.

One further structure of language which exists within Saussure's conception of *langue* concerns the restrictions on *combination* and **substitution** of linguistic elements.

If we take the collection of signs "The cat sat on the mat":

An element such as "cat" can signify because it is different from "mat", "the", "on", "sat", as well as "gibbet", "lorry", "pope", "anthrax" etc., etc.

But look how it combines with other elements.

It can appear in a strict order with "the", "sat", "on" and "mat" to form a **syntagm** (a logically ordered collection of signs, e.g. a sentence, a phrase).

In this sense, then, "cat" has syntagmatic relations with those elements which can precede and succeed it in a sequence.

the   cat   sat

moggy

feline
quadruped

However, signification takes place through something more than linear combinatory relations.

What if there were choices of signs?

on the mat

mped reposed

dog

In this way, "cat" can be said to have **paradigmatic** relations (relations of substitutability) with "feline quadruped" and "moggy".

Such paradigmatic relations must fit in with syntagmatic relations like the x and y axes on a graph.

Yet there is some flexibility, as long as the syntagmatic relations allow it; "cat", for example, might have paradigmatic relations with its opposite, "dog", provided that the syntagm only requires substitution of an animate noun.

17

Charles Sanders Peirce (1839-1914)

Hailed as the foremost American philosopher, Charles Peirce (pronounced "purse") was born into a well-bred academic family in Cambridge, Massachusetts.

This was the world of Harvard College, and Peirce's contemporaries included William James, Chauncey Wright and Oliver Wendell Holmes, Jr.

But Peirce did not lead a model genteel academic life in which he steadily constructed his "semeiotic".

He was a difficult youth, largely as a result of his recurrent neuralgia, a disorder involving acute facial pain and reportedly manifesting itself in outbursts of temper and emotion.

During his undistinguished sojourn at Harvard, Peirce filled a summer placement at the U.S. Coast and Geodetic Survey, an association which was to continue for thirty years, with Peirce making major contributions to geodesy and astronomy.

In spite of this, Peirce was never able to procure the stable academic life that might have enabled him to consolidate his nebulous writing.

He became separated from his wife, Zina Fay, in 1877, eventually divorcing her. In 1883 he married a French woman, Juliette Pourtalai, with whom he had been living before his divorce from Zina. Nowadays, this does not seem a big deal.

BUT ATTITUDES TO DIVORCE IN MY MILIEU WERE STRICT. THE DETAILS OF MY LIVING ARRANGEMENTS PROVIDED AMMUNITION FOR MY ENEMIES.

Along with his argumentativeness, Peirce's unacceptable lifestyle led to the termination of his only post as a university lecturer. After having appointed him to teach logic in 1879, the trustees of Johns Hopkins University initiated Peirce's destruction.

AS IF TO MAKE MATTERS WORSE, AFTER LENGTHY DISPUTES WITH THE COAST SURVEY IN 1891, I FOUND MYSELF EVEN WITHOUT THIS JOB.

For the remainder of his life, in a period of American history in which the rags-to-respectability stories of Horatio Alger existed alongside the social Darwinism of the established classes, Peirce eked out an existence by accepting advances for popular magazine articles.

Yet Peirce left behind him a voluminous series of writings (collected into eight volumes by his editors from 1931-58), many of which were unpublished. It is here that Peirce worked out his logic and philosophy, bounded by what he was to call "semeiotic", his theory of signs.

Beginning with his 1867 paper, "On a New List of Categories", Peirce spent the rest of his life elaborating a **triadic** theory of the sign. Although he confessed a preoccupation with the number 3, it is easy to see that the shape of Peirce's sign makes perfect sense.

UNLIKE SAUSSURE, WHOSE SIGN IS A SELF-CONTAINED DYAD, I INSIST THAT THE SIGN CONSISTS OF A TRIPLE RELATION...

S/R

Representamen
(the sign itself) which has a relation to an **Object**, which relation entails an **Interpretant**

O

I

Peirce

Ceci est un signe

THE SIGN OR REPRESENTAMEN IS, QUITE SIMPLY, SOMETHING WHICH STANDS TO SOMEBODY FOR SOMETHING IN SOME RESPECT OR CAPACITY.

The Object is that which the Sign/Representamen stands for - although it is slightly more complicated than that, because it can be

an Immediate Object

the object as it is *represented* by the sign

a Dynamic Object

the object independent of the sign which leads to the *production* of the sign

The Interpretant is the trickiest of the lot. It is NOT the "interpreter". Rather it is a "proper significate effect".

Most often it is thought of as the sign in the mind that is the result of an encounter with a sign.

This is a good starting place, although it is more accurate to consider the Interpretant as a kind of proper "result". I might point at the sky, for instance, and rather than simply registering the signification of sky, you will look in the direction of the pointing finger.

Thus an Interpretant is produced.

Yet, like an Object, there is more than one kind of Interpretant.

the Immediate Interpretant

which manifests itself in the correct understanding of the sign (e.g. looking at the sky and seeing precisely the star that the finger points to)

the Dynamic Interpretant

which is the direct result of the sign (e.g. looking at the sky in general in response to the pointing finger)

the Final Interpretant

which is the relatively rare result of a sign which functions fully in every instance of its use (e.g. looking at precisely the star that the finger points to and realizing that the pointing finger indicates that the star is specifically Proxima Centauri)

But this is still not the end of the story.

Whereas Saussure's sign (signified/signifier) needs to combine with other signs to take part in the flow of meaning, Peirce's version of signification has an in-built dynamism.

Remember: we said that the Interpretant was like a further sign or "sign in the mind". As such, the Interpretant has an important role to play in the sign triad.

In its guise as Interpretant it is also able to assume the mantle of a further Sign/Representamen.

This places it in a relationship to a further Object which, in turn, entails an Interpretant, which is transformed into a Sign/Representamen which is in relationship to a further Object, effecting another Interpretant, and so on *ad infinitum*.

O

O

R

I/R

O

I/R

I/R

I/R

I/R

O

I/R

O

I/R

I/R

O

I/R

O

O

It is worth remembering this potential when we consider Derrida's relation to semiotics.

This principle of an Interpretant producing further signs is, in everyday terms, quite familiar. We are all aware of how one sign triggers a chain of associations which eventually seem quite removed from the initial sign.

In semiotics, this potential - and it is only a potential, simply because normal practice dictates that we need to go to work, execute chores, go to sleep etc., rather than constantly produce signs - is often referred to as **unlimited semiosis.**

Peirce's view of sign functioning is clearly quite complex when one considers the way, in his semeiotic, in which signs necessarily generate further signs.

Note: A story has it that Schubert, after playing a new piano piece, was asked by a woman what it meant. Schubert said nothing but, in answer, returned to the piano and played the music again. The pure feeling of the music - Firstness - was its point.

But the plot thickens. Peirce's sign does not function on its own but as a manifestation of a general phenomenon. Peirce identified three categories of phenomena which he labelled

Firstness, Secondness and **Thirdness.**

The realm of Firstness is difficult to conceive but is usually understood in terms of "feeling".

Firstness has no relations, it is not to be thought of in opposition to another thing and it is merely a "possibility".

It is like a musical note or a vague taste or a sense of a colour.

Secondness is the realm of brute facts which arise from a relationship.

It is the sense that arises when, in the process of closing a door, it is found that the door is stuck as the result of an object being in its way. The relation is discovered and the world is revealed to be made up of things and their co-existence with other things.

Above all, for Peirce, the crucial category is **Thirdness,** the realm of general laws.

Where Secondness amounts to brutal facts, Thirdness is the mental element.
For Peirce, a Third brings a First into relation with a Second.
As in the analogy of giving, A gives B to C, hence B brings A and C into a relationship.

Transposed onto Peirce's sign triad, the categories result in the following:

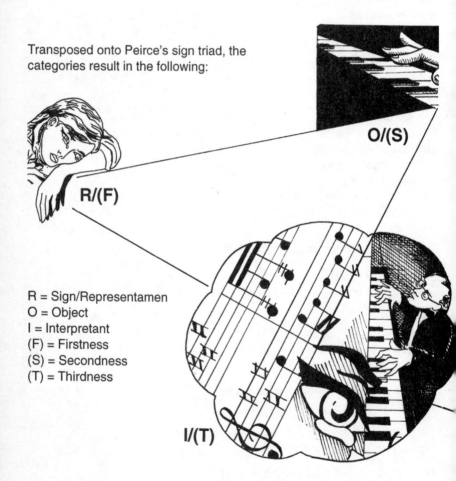

O/(S)

R/(F)

R = Sign/Representamen
O = Object
I = Interpretant
(F) = Firstness
(S) = Secondness
(T) = Thirdness

I/(T)

The Sign or Representamen is a First;
the Object is a Second;
and the Interpretant is a Third.

Note that this is a snapshot of the triad in the possibility of unlimited semiosis.

The Interpretant here represents Thirdness. But the Interpretant becomes a First for the next triad.

As a First, then, the Sign (or Representamen) also acts as a Third, bringing the next Interpretant into a relationship with the Object, or rendering "inefficient relations efficient", establishing "a habit or general rule whereby [signs] will act on occasion".

The reason for mapping the three categories onto the triadic elements Representamen, Object, Interpretant becomes clearer as we consider how Peirce tries to categorize different sign types.

Note: This indicates what Peirce shares with Saussure: a theory of signs as a coded access to an object.

Initially, Peirce posited 10 sign types, which he then revised in order to theorize 66 signs, before eventually coming up with the troublesome figure of 59,049.

It would be difficult to go through all of these; however, we can begin to look at the process by which such sign types might be generated.

If the sign is a triad (Sign/Representamen, Object, Interpretant) then it has three formal aspects, of Firstness, Secondness and Thirdness respectively.

These formal aspects, in turn, bear a relation to the categories (Firstness, Secondness, Thirdness) of existence or phenomena in general.

The interaction of formal aspects of signs and aspects of being can be envisaged in terms of a sign-generating graph.

The rows consist of the categories (Firstness, Secondness, Thirdness) as they relate to each element of the sign triad.

The columns consist of the categories as they relate to being (quality, brute facts, general laws).

This generates signs as follows:

	Quality *Firstness*	Brute facts *Secondness*	Law *Thirdness*
Representamen *Firstness*	Qualisign	Sinsign	Legisign
Object *Secondness*	Icon	Index	Symbol
Interpretant *Thirdness*	Rheme	Dicent	Argument

At the level of the
Sign/Representamen
(i.e. a First)

a Qualisign
(a Representamen made up of a quality,
e.g. the colour green)

a Sinsign
(a Representamen made up of an existing
physical reality, e.g. a road sign in a
specific street)

a Legisign
(a Representamen made up of a law,
e.g. the sound of the referee's whistle in
a football match)

At the level of the Object (i.e. a Second)
an Icon (where the sign relates to its object in some resemblance with it , e.g. a photograph)
I CAN BE ALL THREE.
a Symbol (where the sign relates to its object by means of convention alone, e.g. a word, a flag)
an Index (where the sign relates to its object in terms of causation, e.g. weathercock, medical symptom)

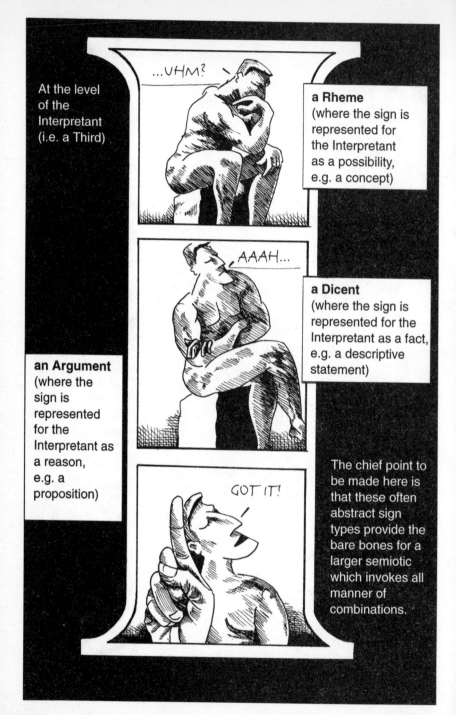

At the level of the Interpretant (i.e. a Third)

a Rheme
(where the sign is represented for the Interpretant as a possibility, e.g. a concept)

...UHM?

AAAH...

a Dicent
(where the sign is represented for the Interpretant as a fact, e.g. a descriptive statement)

an Argument
(where the sign is represented for the Interpretant as a reason, e.g. a proposition)

GOT IT!

The chief point to be made here is that these often abstract sign types provide the bare bones for a larger semiotic which invokes all manner of combinations.

Here is one example of such a combination:

A football referee shows a red card to a football player who has committed a blatant professional foul. As the red card invokes rules (professional fouls are illegal and lead to penalties against the perpetrator), it is an Argument. It is also Symbolic (the red card signifies the professional foul by convention), and therefore also a Legisign (a general law).

But the red card has been used by referees before, and players know this well enough. Therefore, this instance of the use of the red card acts as a brute fact, and as such is a Dicent Indexical Sinsign (a statement, caused by the action of the referee, of the facts of football protocol).

THE DICENT INDEXICAL SINSIGN IS THEREFORE A REPLICA OF THE ARGUMENT-SYMBOL-LEGISIGN.

The work of Peirce and Saussure provides the most obvious reference point for semiotics in the twentieth century.

But there is a link with the past that both thinkers represent.

I MAKE THE STRUCTURE OF LANGUAGE ('LANGUE') THE STARTING POINT FOR ANY PROJECTED STUDY OF SIGNS.

I DEVISE A SEMEIOTIC WHICH EMBRACES BOTH "NATURAL" AND "CONVENTIONAL" SIGNS OF ALL KINDS.

VARNISH

JOHN LOCKE
WILLIAM OF OCKHAM
ST. AUGUSTINE

PLATO
ARISTOTLE
THE STOICS
PHILOSOPHERS OF
THE MIDDLE AGES
THOMAS HOBBES
JOHN LOCKE
THOMAS REID

HUMAN SIGNS AND DISCOURSE

THE UNIVERSE PERFUSED WITH SIGNS

KRISTEVA · BAUDRILLARD
FOUCAULT · DERRIDA
LÉVI-STRAUSS
BARTHES

RICHARDS · MORRIS
OGDEN · FISCH
SEBEOK

And as Peirce and Saussure have their forebears, they have also spawned successors.

SAUSSURE

PEIRCE

JAKOBSON

ECO

Saussure and Semiology

One of the most penetrating critiques of Saussure acts as evidence of the spread of his influence.

The Soviet theorist, **Valentin Vološinov** (1895-1936), names the school of Saussure as a key player in Russian linguistics. However, he chides it for its "abstract objectivism": that is to say, he disagrees that *langue* (used by all, yet intangible) is where we might find the true social nature of communication.

> I DEMAND THAT THE FOCUS OF LANGUAGE STUDY SHOULD BE THE UTTERANCE ("PAROLE"), WHICH IS FIXED IN A SPECIFIC SITUATION AND CHANGES AS THE SITUATION DOES.

*It is widely believed that Vološinov was actually the Russian scholar, **Mikhail Bakhtin** (1895-1975).*

This argument is important for the development of semiotics and we will return to it again.

For the European thinkers that follow Saussure, however, the concept of *langue* represents the major breakthrough.

A Danish linguist, **Louis Hjelmslev** (1899-1965), embarked on Saussure's task of forging "a science that studies the life of signs within society". The crucial first move in this project involved the promotion of *langue* to the level of a master system of signs that governed *all* sign production above and beyond that described by linguistics alone.

ALL SIGNS ARE SUBORDINATE TO A HIGHER PRINCIPLE OF ORGANIZATION THAN THAT OF THEIR OWN LOCAL SYSTEM.

Allied to this is an extension of Saussure's understanding of individual sign-functioning.

Where Saussure's sign (comprising the internal relations of signified and signifier) operates in a dimension where its job is to **denote**, Hjelmslev suggests that the sign also has a further dimension.

ORGANIZED AND INCORPORATED INTO THIS OTHER DIMENSION OF THE SIGN IS A MASS OF INFORMATION WHICH COMES FROM OUTSIDE THE SIGN ITSELF.

Not only does the sign contain a relation between a material substance (signifier) and a mental concept (signified), it also contains a relation between itself and systems of signs **outside itself**.

MANIFEST DESTINY

If we take a sign such as "manifest destiny", the dimension that Hjelmslev is describing becomes much clearer.

It is relatively easy to identify the signifiers that are in use in this sign; similarly, one can analyze the two words in order to work out a straightforward **denotative** meaning for them (e.g. that a predetermined course of events is obvious).

BUT, AS IN THE CASE OF MANY SIGNS, THERE IS SOMETHING THAT THIS KIND OF ANALYSIS SEEMS TO BE MISSING.

THE PHRASE HAS SOME FAIRLY SPECIFIC CONNECTIONS TO THE TIME AND MILIEU IN WHICH IT WAS USED.

What strikes the reader of these two words - if he or she is sufficiently versed in history - is a whole set of associations to do with American expansion (the frontier, the 19th century, heroic pioneers, the railroad, the claiming of land from the East to the Pacific, the removal of Native Americans).

"Manifest destiny", coined in 1845, was a cliché used by successive U.S. presidents in the 19th century to refer to and justify the colonization of a continent.

The sign, then, can be said to have the power of **connotation**.
Like all signs, it can - potentially - invoke the action of existing sign-systems.

AS AMERICA'S TERRITORY SPREADS, SO WILL DEMOCRACY!

MANIFEST DESTINY

Connotation is by no means an unfamiliar phenomenon.

In fact, probably one of the most gifted and entertaining analysts of connotation presented his most famous insights into signs *before* becoming immersed in semiology.

I HOPE TO ACCOUNT IN DETAIL FOR THE MYSTIFICATION WHICH TRANSFORMS PETIT-BOURGEOIS CULTURE INTO A UNIVERSAL NATURE.

From 1954-56, a series of essays appeared in a French magazine, *Les Lettres nouvelles*. In each one, their author, **Roland Barthes** (1915-80), set out to expose a "Mythology of the Month", largely by showing how the denotations in the signs of popular culture betray connotations which are themselves "myths" generated by the larger sign system that makes up society.

The book which contains these essays - appropriately entitled *Mythologies* and published in 1957 - presents meditations on striptease, the New Citroën, the foam that is a product of detergents, the face of Greta Garbo, steak and chips, and so on.

In each essay, Barthes takes a seemingly unnoticed phenomenon from everyday living and spends time deconstructing it, showing how the "obvious" connotations which it carries have usually been carefully constructed.

IN "THE WORLD OF WRESTLING" I DESCRIBE HOW, FAR FROM BEING A SPORT, WRESTLING IS A COMPLEX SPECTACLE OF SIGNS MADE UP OF THE WRESTLERS' BODIES AND EXCESSIVE GESTURES.

Even though everybody knows that wrestling is "fixed" it does not stop people (often old ladies) getting carried away with certain bouts.

More subtly, in "The Romans in Films", Barthes shows that the means by which connotations of "Roman-ness" are produced in Joseph Mankiewicz's film of *Julius Caesar* are minute.

Apart from the obvious things (togas, sandals, swords etc.), Barthes notes that all the characters are wearing fringes.

EVEN THOSE WHO HAVE LITTLE HAIR HAVE NOT BEEN LET OFF FOR ALL THAT, AND THE HAIRDRESSER - THE KING-PIN OF THE FILM - HAS STILL MANAGED TO PRODUCE ONE LAST LOCK WHICH DULY REACHES THE TOP OF THE FOREHEAD, ONE OF THOSE ROMAN FOREHEADS, WHOSE SMALLNESS HAS AT ALL TIMES INDICATED A SPECIFIC MIXTURE OF SELF-RIGHTEOUSNESS, VIRTUE AND CONQUEST.

It is probably these semiotic analyses of Barthes that are the most popularly known, and which form the basis of the kind of conversations in cinema foyers and on late night arts programmes to which we made reference at the beginning of this book.

But Barthes does much more than graft quasi-technical jargon onto popular artefacts. He reads phenomena closely; and in his deconstructions he pays deliberate attention to the complexities which maintain certain constructions.

CARS ARE BETTER THAN PUBLIC TRANSPORT

HOMOSEXUALITY IS UNNATURAL

MEAT MAKES YOU STRONG

SUPERMARKETS MAKE LIFE EASIER

SURGERY SAVES LIVES

LESBIANS ARE UGLY

SEAN CONNERY WAS THE BEST JAMES BOND

9 OUT OF 10 CATS PREFER FISH

THE "MYTHS" WHICH SUFFUSE OUR LIVES ARE INSIDIOUS PRECISELY BECAUSE THEY APPEAR SO NATURAL. THEY CALL OUT FOR THE DETAILED ANALYSIS WHICH SEMIOTICS CAN DELIVER.

Take Barthes' 1964 essay, "The Rhetoric of the Image". Here he analyzes an ad for Panzani pasta which consists of a simple photograph of some basic ingredients (tomatoes, mushrooms, peppers), some packets of pasta and some tins of sauce, hanging out of a string bag.

He separates the ad into three messages:

a "linguistic" message	- all the words in the ad
a "coded iconic" message	- the connotations (derived from the larger sign system of society) in the photograph
a "non-coded iconic" message	- the denotations in the photograph

The linguistic message
The key thing about this is the peculiar assonance found in the word "Panzani". This **denotes** the name of the product but, coupled with such linguistic signs as "L'Italienne", it also **connotes** the general idea of "Italianicity".

The coded iconic message
These are the visual connotations derived from the arrangement of photographed elements.

Among these are:

PATES - SAUCE - PARMESAN
A L'ITALIENNE DE LUXE

freshness (of natural ingredients as well as, by association, packaged ones)

a return from market

a trawl (string bag = fishing net)

a still life

Italianicity (the tri-coloured hues of the natural ingredients and the packet labels = Italian flag)

The non-coded iconic message
Barthes uses this term to refer to the "literal" denotation, the recognition of identifiable objects in the photograph, irrespective of the larger societal code (or *langue*).

It is significant that Barthes should pick this particular order for his three messages.

The linguistic message may be the one that spectators of the photograph look for first in an advertisement of this kind.

THE WORDS AT THE BOTTOM OF PICTORIAL ADS - WHAT I CALL THE "ANCHORAGE" - OFTEN PROVIDE CRUCIAL INFORMATION ABOUT WHAT THE PRODUCT DOES OR IS.

More problematic is the relationship between the two "iconic" messages: one "coded"/connotative and the other "non-coded"/denotative.

Barthes discusses the connotative first because, as he argues, the process of connotation is so "natural" and so immediate when it is experienced that it is almost impossible to separate denotation and connotation.

The identification of denotation only takes place when connotation is theoretically *deleted* from the equation.

Logically, a reader recognizes what signs actually depict and then goes on to decipher some sort of cultural, social or emotional meaning.

In reality, however, identification of what signs depict - especially pictorial ones - happens so quickly that it is easy to forget that it has happened at all.

One other important area which Barthes opens up for the study of signs is the role of the reader.

Connotation, although it is a feature of the sign, requires the activity of a reader in order to take place.

Taking his cue from Hjelmslev, Barthes therefore produces his map of sign functioning:

1. signifier	2. signified
3. denotative sign	
4. CONNOTATIVE SIGNIFIER	5. CONNOTATIVE SIGNIFIED
6. CONNOTATIVE SIGN	

The denotative sign (3) is made up of a signifier (1) and signified (2). But the denotative sign is also a connotative signifier (4).

That is to say, it is a material substance: only if you are in possession of the sign "lion" is it then possible to have connotations of its pride, ferocity, courage etc.

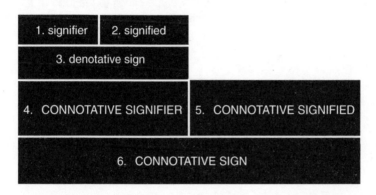

And a connotative signifier must engender a connotative signified (5) to produce a connotative sign (6).

This is where the kind of systematic approach to signs that Barthes wished to pursue becomes very problematic.

On the one hand, following Hjelmslev, he clings to the idea of a large system or code or *langue* or societal signs.

BUT I ADMIT THAT WHILE INDIVIDUAL INSTANCES OF SIGNS WILL REDUCE THE "ANARCHIC" TENDENCY TO ENDLESS MEANINGS, THE CULTURAL DIVERSITY AND CONSTANT CHANGE THAT MAKES UP THE REALM OF THE CONNOTATIVE SIGNIFIED IS GLOBAL AND DIFFUSE.

Barthes was not alone in pondering these dilemmas. In the 1950s and 1960s he formed part of the influential intellectual current which is usually known as **structuralism**.

Based on Saussure's call for a science of signs, structuralism embraced semiology but often seemed to go beyond the strict remit of sign functioning. In fact, the chief structuralist associated with Gallic intellectual life was an anthropologist, **Claude Lévi-Strauss** (b.1908).

Amalgamating aspects of the work of the Russian-born Prague linguist, **Roman Jakobson** (1896-1982), Saussurean linguistics and the Freudian unconscious, Lévi-Strauss demonstrated both the complexity and the highly patterned nature of the "savage mind".

The constituent bridge between Lévi-Strauss' anthropology and semiological principles is the notion of **structure**.

What his voluminous field research on totemism, ritual, kinship patterns and, especially, myth, demonstrates is a correlation between cultural artefacts which is analogous to relations within language.

THE ERROR OF TRADITIONAL ANTHROPOLOGY, LIKE THAT OF TRADITIONAL LINGUISTICS, WAS TO CONSIDER THE TERMS, AND NOT THE **RELATIONS** BETWEEN THE TERMS.

This is a very Saussurean perspective.
Firstly, it sees any manifestation of culture as part of a larger system.
But, secondly - and more important - it considers individual items in culture not as items with intrinsic identities but as significant in relation to their place in the structure.

By **value** he means that signs, like other things with value, can

IN THE 'COURS' I WAS VERY CAREFUL TO AVOID REFERRING TO "MEANING". INSTEAD, I REFER TO THE RELATIONSHIP BETWEEN SIGNS AS **VALUE**.

a) be *exchanged* for something *dissimilar*

b) be **compared** with **similar** things

Take a £1 coin. This can

a) be exchanged for bread, beer, newspapers, etc.

Also, it can

b) be compared to a $5 bill

Similarly, a word can be exchanged for an idea or compared with another word.

55

What Saussure is getting at is that the items in question do not have intrinsic identities. In fact, it may be that the £1 coin is physically made up of alloys that cost just 37p in total.

However, the coin's role in the system is to enact the value of £1 in relation to other items of currency (20p, 50p, £5 notes etc.) and other commodities (£1's worth of bread, beer etc.).

For Saussure, it is value which generates the **system of differences** that is *langue*.

At the lowest stratum of language there are various fundamental sounds which linguists call **phonemes**.

In the word /dog/ there are three phonemes: /d/, /o/ and /g/.

It would be madness to suggest that the /d/ phoneme is somehow more important than the /g/ phoneme, or that one is a positive term and the other is not.

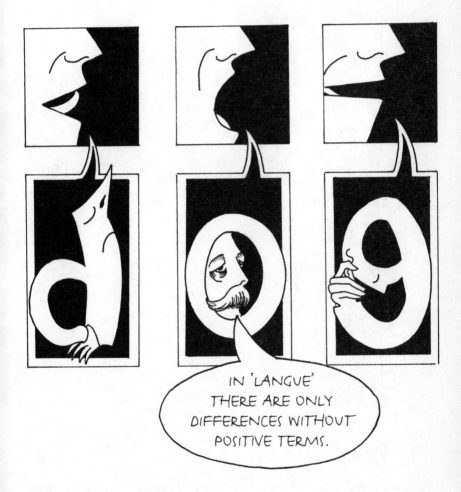

When this principle is elevated to the level of wider systems such as those that exist in cultures, we can see how the notion of a **structure** of relations or differences becomes very important.

As a preliminary example, let us take a street in London.

The Elephant and Castle was for many years the point where six roads met, and its buildings were arranged along the course of the converging routes. Then, in the 1960s, to ease traffic congestion, everything was swept away and a new junction was superimposed over the old building lines.

The junction itself was now the focal point of the Elephant and Castle.

So, if this place has experienced such a radical change of identity, why does it still go by the name of Elephant and Castle?

Because it is part of a **structure** or **system.**

Elephant and Castle has remained as such because of its relationship to adjacent streets such as New Kent Road, Newington Causeway, London Road, St George's Road, etc.

It is part of a structure known as the London road system which allows relations of access to vehicles delivering services or goods.

It is one of many veins in relation to **different** veins and arteries in a body which accommodates traffic flow.

This structuralist evaluation of a London street is similar to the kind of work carried out by Lévi-Strauss and others allied to semiology in the 50s and 60s.

For Lévi-Strauss, anthropological phenomena such as kinship systems can be studied as meaningful in their structural relations. The prohibitions on marriage which exist in certain societies - the most obvious is the taboo on incest - are not the result of simple biological predeterminations.
Instead, they represent a **signifying** or **cultural** system.

YOU CAN'T MARRY YOUR SISTER. HOW ABOUT MARRYING YOUR COUSIN? THAT WOULD BE A NICE COMBINATION.

In certain societies, Lévi-Strauss argues, who marries whom is bound by a meaningful system of exchange, possibility and difference which is not dissimilar to the rules enshrined in language.

The Structure of Myth

In the myths of a society, similar rules apply. A **structure** is a model of operations that allows for subsequent transformations of myths, while still conforming to the structure's ground rules.

Myth relates the same story again and again with relatively superficial transformation of the elements which make up that story. Let's take the example of the Oedipus family myth.

Cadmos, the ancestor of Oedipus and founder of the city of Thebes, killed a dragon. From its teeth, which Cadmos planted in the earth, sprang up the Sparti warriors, who at once began to kill each other. The five survivors became the ancestors of the Thebans.

Later on, we also find Oedipus killing an earth monster, the riddling Sphinx. For this, Oedipus is rewarded with the throne of Thebes - vacant since the recent death of King Laios - and he marries the widowed Queen Jocasta. In fact, Oedipus had unknowingly murdered his own father, King Laios, and married his mother. Thebes is punished by a plague for these two unknown crimes.

After the exile of Oedipus, his two sons, Eteocles and Polyneices, kill each other in a fight for the throne. The senate of Thebes decrees that the corpse of Polyneices is to be left unburied, but his sister Antigone disobeys by performing funeral rites for him. For this she was condemned to be buried alive.

It is interesting, too, that the name of Oedipus' grandfather, Labdacos, suggests *lame,* that of Laios his father, *left-sided,* and Oedipus itself means *swollen foot* - all names which imply "not walking straight".

Structure and Mythemes

Lévi-Strauss establishes the structure of myths, such as that of Oedipus, by breaking them down into their smallest possible constituents, which he calls **mythemes** (not unlike linguistic phonemes). Mythemes are envisaged as "bundles of relations". Lévi-Strauss disregards the narrative, where one action follows another, and instead rearranges myths so that types of relations - the mythemes - are placed in groups with one another. For instance, the bundle "Cadmos kills the dragon" is of the same group as "Oedipus kills the sphinx".

In the following analysis, the Oedipus myth is arranged into columns of grouped **mythemes** and rows of **narrative sequence**.

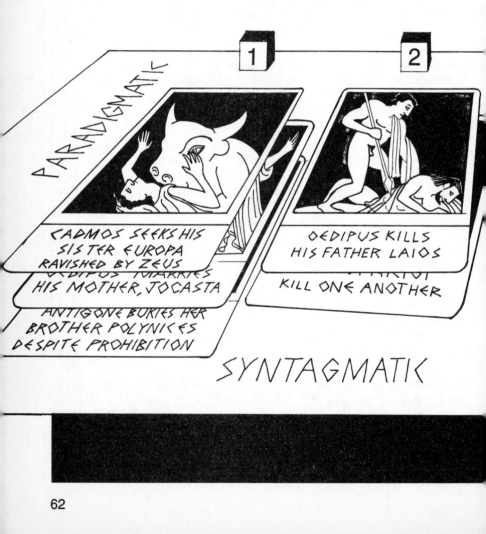

PARADIGMATIC

1

2

CADMOS SEEKS HIS SISTER EUROPA RAVISHED BY ZEUS

OEDIPUS KILLS HIS FATHER LAIOS

OEDIPUS MARRIES HIS MOTHER, JOCASTA

...KILL ONE ANOTHER

ANTIGONE BURIES HER BROTHER POLYNICES DESPITE PROHIBITION

SYNTAGMATIC

Effecctively, this presents a syntagmatic axis (narrative sequence, horizontally) and a paradigmatic axis (bundles of relations, vertically).

The purpose of this rewriting is not for Lévi-Strauss to get at the final meaning of the myth; rather he wishes to show the conditions of the myth's production and transformation.

The relations are as follows:

Column 1 - over-rating of blood relations
Column 2 - under-rating of blood relations (i.e. inverse of Column 1)
Column 3 - slaying of monsters
Column 4 - difficulty of balance and standing (in the names)

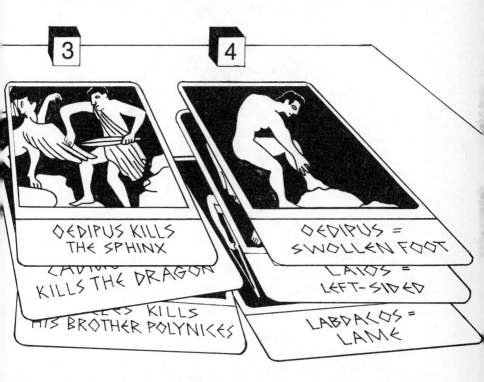

For Lévi-Strauss the myth enacts an almost universal concern with human origins. Does humankind come from Earth/Blood or from reproduction of humans?

After the over-rating of blood and its inverse, the monster - an Earth/Blood creature - is slain. The imbalance and inability to stand in the male protagonists' names is the reference to the birth of humans (who cannot stand until they achieve balance and strength).

But in numerous other myths, the human that cannot stand is born of Earth.

The four columns therefore represent the conditions of asking, as well as the contradictory positions entailed by, the question of human origins.

In a sense, the semiotic relations between elements of the Oedipus myth actually signal some kind of message about the nature of myths in general, particularly those to do with human origins.

FACULTE DES LETTRES

For European intellectuals, Lévi-Strauss' bold observations about so-called "primitive" societies opened up a whole new dimension to the understanding of cultures in general.

His formulations regarding myth contributed to those structuralist studies of textual phenomena which loosely constituted the Paris School in the 1960s.

In the field of analysing narrative structures, Lévi-Strauss' work prefigures and overlaps with that of **Algirdas Julien Greimas** (1917-92) and **Claude Brémond** (b. 1929).

During the same period, *Communications*, a Paris journal dealing largely with the image, published a great deal of influential structuralist work, including Roland Barthes on photography, **Christian Metz** (1931-93) on cinema and **Tzvetan Todorov** (b. 1939) on poetics.

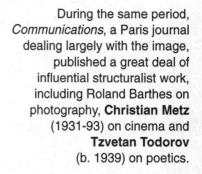

Structuralism

In fact, "structuralism", as a synonym for semiological analysis, became very much *en vogue*. In 1967, the French literary journal *Quinzaine Littéraire* published a much-reproduced cartoon which depicted the leading proponents of structuralism dressed in grass skirts amidst rich foliage.

A young **Michel Foucault** (1926-84) cheerfully lectures to his audience: the psychoanalyst **Jacques Lacan** (1901-81), sitting cross-legged with folded arms, Lévi-Strauss (taking field notes as usual), and Roland Barthes (pensive expression but relaxed of body).

Most commentators agree that the "primitive" surroundings signal the dominance of Lévi-Strauss and his anthropological bent. More importantly, perhaps, is the way in which the cartoon presages the realm beyond textuality heralded by a new wave of semiologically implicated thinking.

Post-structuralism

The project of a post-structuralist semiotics (or semiology) cannot really be placed firmly in time. Moreover, the term "post-structuralism" is one which is rarely used in France, its putative place of origin.

Nevertheless, most commentators agree that post-structuralism's origins are most recognizable in the years immediately preceding the student uprisings of May 1968.

ÉCRITURE et DIFFÉRENCE

Possibly one of the key formative moments, then, is the appearance of Jacques Lacan's *Écrits* and the extraordinary publication of three books in one year (1967) by the Algerian-born French philosopher, **Jacques Derrida** (b. 1930).

One of these latter, a collection of essays entitled *Écriture et différence*, quite clearly represents a revolt against Lévi-Strauss and structuralism, and serves also as the opening salvo in Derrida's barrage aimed at Western philosophy in general.

Central to the post-structuralist critique is a concern with the role of the human subject in signification.

Structuralist semiology had basically treated the subject as the "bearer" of structures. Far from being the locus of agency, the human was understood as dominated by kinship norms, narrative processes, myths, gender relations or whatever structure was under discussion.

In this sense, structuralist semiology was "anti-humanist" in its orientation, and often bleakly so at that.

If one reads the work of the Marxist philosopher **Louis Althusser** (1918-90) and the early books of Michel Foucault - both of whom had an oblique relation to structuralism at this time - the outlook for humanity looks grim indeed.

May '68 effectively stirred up the pot of post-structuralist semiotics.

The location of structuralism's main champions in the establishment Grande Écoles meant that, by association, they could come to represent the rigidity in education against which many students rebelled.

More importantly, however, the agency and the interventionism on the part of students and striking workers which seemingly brought France so close to revolution was radically at odds with the restrictive "anti-humanism" of structuralist teachings.

CLEARLY THERE WAS A NEED TO UNDERSTAND SUBJECTIVITY AS **MORE** THAN THE PRODUCT OF THOROUGH DOMINATION BY THE SYSTEM AND **LESS** THAN PURE AGENCY.

YET THE REVOLUTION FAILED.

FACULTE DES LETTRES

MAY 68

Saussure's concept of *langue* rendered the user of language as just one junction in the circulation of differences between signs.

Logically, it seemed that the storehouse or cupboard of differences remained open all hours for the subject or language user to come along and assemble utterances.

I AM NOT CONCERNED TO GIVE ANY SENSE OF WHY, BEYOND THE NEED TO COMMUNICATE, ANY SUBJECT WOULD USE THE SYSTEM IN A PARTICULAR WAY.

The sign was conceived instead as an arbitrary notation for referring to the mental concepts already harboured by the potential sign user.

As such, the human's relation to the system was based largely on "functionalist" convenience.

The way in which post-structuralism understands sign users is very different.

As early as 1939, the eminent French linguist **Émile Benveniste** (1902-76) expressed his misgivings regarding the "arbitrariness" of relations in the Saussurean sign.

His comments would be significant for theorizing semiological subjects.

THE CONNECTION BETWEEN THE SIGNIFIER (THE MATERIAL NOTATION) AND THE SIGNIFIED (MENTAL CONCEPT ENGENDERED BY THE SIGNIFIER) IS SO COMPREHENSIVELY LEARNED AT AN EARLY AGE BY SIGN USERS THAT VIRTUALLY NO SEPARATION BETWEEN THE TWO IS EVER EXPERIENCED.

71

Put another way, the word "tree" for English speakers provokes a mental concept of "treeness" with such immediacy that it feels as if the process of connecting a signifier to a signified has not even happened.

What goes on in the mind is instant, and rather than an "arbitrary" connection occurring there, for Benveniste the link between signified and signifier is **necessary**.

However, there *is* an arbitrary relationship in the signifying process. This occurs between the whole sign (signified and signifier) and the **thing in the real world**.

Why is this important?

TREE

Consider this: The word "I" is used by the whole of a linguistic community. It is used by individuals to refer to themselves instead of using a proper name (e.g. John Smith).

So, for Saussure, "I" is surely a sign which contains an arbitrary relation between signifier and signified.

> "I", THEREFORE, IS NOT ME; TO USE "I" IS SIMPLY TO SUBSCRIBE TO A SYSTEM OF SIGNIFYING WHICH EXISTS OUTSIDE ONESELF, TO USE TERMS FROM A COMMUNALLY OWNED STORE.

And that store contains many other terms, each of which has attached to it a fixed concept.

But "I" does not possess this fixed concept or signified. On the contrary, "I" means something different each time it is used in an utterance. It refers to the person using the category "I".

More important than this, however, is the fact that although the use of "I" is effectively a subscription to the language system, it feels as though it isn't.

Following Benveniste, "I" is a sign whose internal relations are **necessary**.

WHEN ONE USES THE WORD "I", IT FEELS AS THOUGH ONE IS ACTUALLY REFERRING TO THE "REAL ME".

But one isn't.

"I" is simply a linguistic category; it doesn't look like me, it doesn't walk like me, it doesn't register how thirsty I am. In short, it can never capture the fullness of me.

There may be an example of *parole* that I utter, such as "I like bananas".

But the "I" in that instance of *parole* that likes bananas is not the same as the person who utters the *parole* (who also likes apples, oranges, grapes, and in fact doesn't really like bananas but was just saying s/he did).

I LIKE BANANAS.

I DON'T, REALLY.

The relation between the subject
and the signifying system, then, is a complex one.

When using linguistic signs, the relationship between signified and
signifier is so entrenched (necessary, almost like second nature) it
seems to the language user that s/he is very close to language.

But, in actual fact, the linguistic system is *outside* the human subject.
The language user is radically separated from the system of signs.
What that system enables the language user to express is a long way
from what s/he actually *feels*.

For example, the subject may be able to express that s/he likes
bananas and, logically, this might fit with all the other predilections that
s/he can express about her/himself.

But there are things which s/he cannot express. for example, an unconscious dislike of bananas.

For Jacques Lacan, this is a crucial factor in demonstrating how the human subject is at once divorced from his/her means of representation but at the same time is *constituted as a subject* by that means of representation.

Taking Saussure's diagram or "algorithm" of signified/signifier, Lacan shows how it presupposes a human relationship to the sign.

me

"I"   ME   *me*

ME

$$\frac{\text{signified}}{\text{signifier}}$$

"I"

The concept (signified) has primacy and stands at the top of the algorithm; the substance (signifier) is secondary and lies at the bottom. The arrows suggest the inseparability of the two, whereby the signifier incites a signified and the signified demands a signifier.

"I"

me

The human relation involved in this version of the sign is one where a "pure" signified exists within the mind of the sign user.

This signified is a kind of idea which is completely untrammelled by mediation. It also seems to be seductively logical that a child, for instance, gains a concept of what a cat is (miaows, eats fish, scratches, etc.), only to be told later by an adult that the entity in question is named "cat".

Lacan takes Saussure's map of the sign and inverts it.

Instead of a pure signified, Lacan presents a mental concept which is completely the result of already existent mediation.

The argument makes more sense if a solid example is used. Lacan chooses the doors of two public toilets which appear as follows:

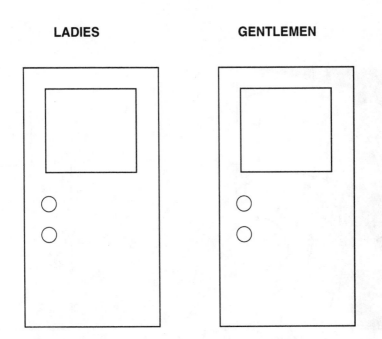

LADIES   **GENTLEMEN**

Presented like this, the doors look like diagrams of the sign as conceived by Saussure.

A closer scrutiny reveals that the doors are identical and the notation attached to each appears at the top of the diagram.

Considered yet further, the difference between the two doors (which appear identical) is not created by anything intrinsic; rather, it is created by the differing signifiers that hang over the doors.

An individual standing before these two doors will derive from the signifiers above a fairly defined conception of what lies behind them.

And when one thinks of what the signifiers in each case engender, the process is pretty important. The difference between "Ladies" and "Gentlemen" allows members of Western civilization to observe a serious cultural law.

LADIES   **GENT**

As Lacan observes, it is the law of "urinary segregation" whereby people of differing gender answer the call of nature when away from home.

Avoiding the embarrassing, offensive and possibly dangerous mistake of choosing the wrong door when seeking to relieve oneself therefore rests on the defining difference of two signifiers.

This is relevant to our earlier developmental analogy.

THE CHILD WHO ACQUIRES THE CONCEPT OF "CAT" DOES SO BECAUSE "CAT" APPEARS AS ONE PRE-EXISTING ELEMENT IN THE WHOLE EDIFICE OF 'LANGUE' WHICH ITSELF PRECEDES THE BIRTH OF INDIVIDUAL HUMANS.

81

In order to take up its place in the world, the child must also take up a position in language.

In order to become a subject and be able to refer to him/herself in the social world, the human must enter into and acquire the pre-existing means of signification.

In this way, Lacan sees the human subject as dominated by the signifier, or more accurately, the differences in *langue.*

His new formulation of the algorithm is thus: $\frac{S}{s}$

Importantly, however, it works like this:

What we have here is not just a picture of the entry of the human being into language.

It is, in fact, the entry of the human into the very stuff of subjectivity.

And of what does that subjectivity consist?

Being enmeshed in the endless web of signification.

THE SIGN IS NOT SELF-CONTAINED, WITH MOVEMENT FROM SIGNIFIED TO SIGNIFIER. IT IS, RATHER, COMPOSED OF TWO DISTINCT REALMS WHICH NEVER MEET.

There is the realm of the big "**S**" (the signifier, the world of operation of signification, culture)...

...and the realm of the small "s" (the inner world or that which cannot be expressed through signification).

Separating them is an impenetrable bar. There is no movement vertically, from signifier to signified. The movement takes place horizontally, with signifieds alighting beneath constantly differing signifiers.

In this sense, then, the signified is far from being pure: it is ethereal, elusive and slippery (one reason for the material register to be marked by a big "S" as opposed
to the hardly
graspable little "s").

But all this does not mean that the subject is caught up in an endless play which makes saying or doing anything meaningful a complete sham.

Lacan calls key signifiers *points de capiton*, or "upholstery buttons" as on a piece of furniture.

The *points de capiton* in a series of signs can operate both synchronically and diachronically.

Diachronically, as a sentence, syntagm or piece of discourse unfolds, each sign will modify the sign which precedes it. Meaning will therefore be retroactively constructed and "sealed" as a *point de capiton* at the crucial endpoint of the syntagm.

Synchronically, the registers S/s in a sign become "sealed" or anchored together as a *point de capiton* in such a way that the sign seems to have an always existing meaning but, in fact, this has been constructed from without.

Often this construction takes place in terms of a "key" or "master" signifier whose power is enhanced by its retroactive thrust.

A common example of this is the "sealing" of a word in political discourse.

THE RIGHT
FREEDOM

FREEDOM
THE END OF

This formulation of the relationship between sign systems and subjectivity is clearly very important.

The signifier "freedom" was constantly "sealed" in Thatcherite Britain during the 1980s in a very characteristic fashion, as a result of the work of those signifiers with which it was juxtaposed and those "master" signifiers which worked upon it.

EXPLOIT WORKERS

TO IGNORE TRADE UNION

TO PAY FOR HEALTH

EDUCATION

FREEDOM

COUNCIL HOUSING

EQUAL

Undoubtedly, Lacan pursued semiological topics primarily for the purpose of broadening his psychoanalytic practice and theory; however, his observations on the functioning of sign systems are incisive enough to demonstrate just how imperative the study of the sign is in modern life.

Although the subject is slightly less clearly implicated in the revision of semiology by Jacques Derrida, there are definite consequences in his work for the human's relation to the system of representation.

His critique of Saussure forms part of an assault on virtually all the major philosophers in the West since Plato, who, according to Derrida, have committed the fatal error of **logocentrism** (the supposed rational power of the word to explain the world).

What Derrida demonstrates about textuality seriously threatens the whole project of "rational" thought.

Central to this threat is the concept of **_différance._**

As a term, this has clear echoes of Saussure's insistence on **difference** as the principle which underpins *langue.* But, for Derrida, Saussure's difference does not go far enough and simply is not true to itself.

Derrida establishes this fact by means of a very astute ruse. Rather than accepting the *Cours* as it was popularized in French intellectual circles during the 1950s and 1960s, he goes back to Saussure's text and interrogates those parts that have largely been neglected.

At various stages in the *Cours* (including one whole chapter), Saussure has a number of things to say about writing, as opposed to his primary object of study, speech.

Chief among these is the recurring motif of writing as a "secondary" form of signification.

Curiously, when Saussure is using writing to illustrate points he is making about speech, he treats them as analogous systems of arbitrary signs. He states that the letter "t", for example, only functions as such when its notation is distinct from all the other written letters.

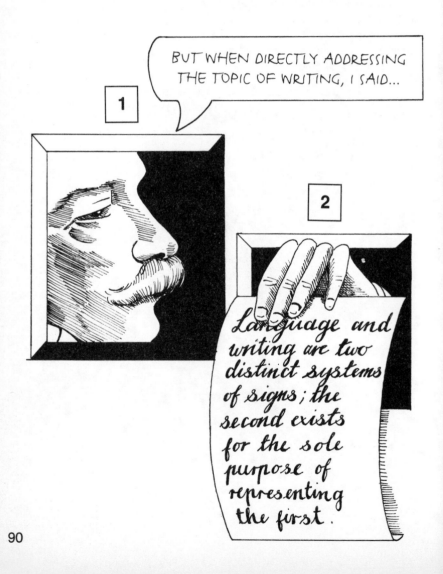

BUT WHEN DIRECTLY ADDRESSING THE TOPIC OF WRITING, I SAID...

1

2

Language and writing are two distinct systems of signs; the second exists for the sole purpose of representing the first.

In short, what Saussure does, according to Derrida, is to **privilege** speech over writing by giving the impression that the spoken signifier is somehow closer to the signified.

> THE SPOKEN FORM ALONE CONSTITUTES THE OBJECT [OF LINGUISTICS].

From the outset, of course, Saussure formulates the signified as a kind of "thought-sound".

As such, then, writing is outside, feeding off the primary essence of signification.

For Derrida, this is damning evidence of Saussure's logocentric tendencies. As with the bulk of Western philosophy since Plato, we are presented with a scenario of **purity** (the spoken sign which contains the signified) invaded by the contaminating force of **mediation** (writing, a secondary system).

91

Instead of getting so upset about contamination, Derrida urges us to live with it.

MEDIATION, LIKE IT OR NOT, IS A WAY OF LIFE.

If Saussure really did believe in the principle of difference - and, moreover, if he was forthrightly promoting a general semiology - he would hail both speech *and* writing as systems of difference.

But, clearly, Saussure is most interested in the idea that the flow of difference can be halted - especially in spoken signs - and there can be access to a stable concept which the signifier designates.

TRANSCENDENTAL SIGNIFIED

Derrida calls this impossible stable concept the **"transcendental signified"**.

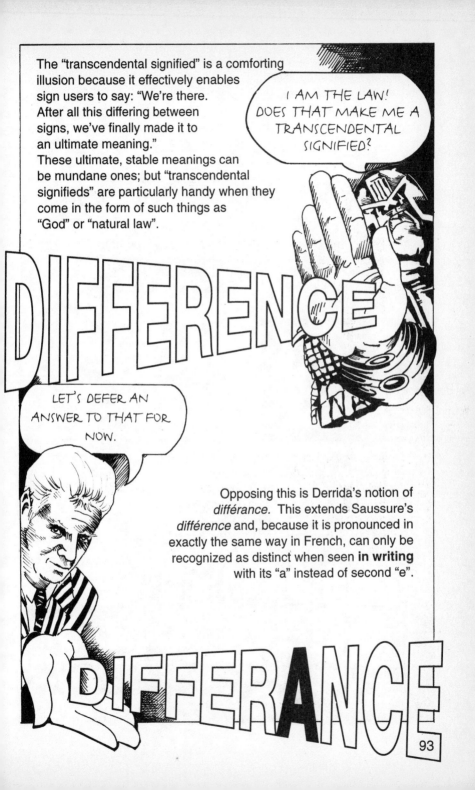

The "transcendental signified" is a comforting illusion because it effectively enables sign users to say: "We're there. After all this differing between signs, we've finally made it to an ultimate meaning."

These ultimate, stable meanings can be mundane ones; but "transcendental signifieds" are particularly handy when they come in the form of such things as "God" or "natural law".

I AM THE LAW! DOES THAT MAKE ME A TRANSCENDENTAL SIGNIFIED?

DIFFERENCE

LET'S DEFER AN ANSWER TO THAT FOR NOW.

Opposing this is Derrida's notion of *différance*. This extends Saussure's *différence* and, because it is pronounced in exactly the same way in French, can only be recognized as distinct when seen **in writing** with its "a" instead of second "e".

DIFFERANCE

The value of a sign derives from the fact that it is different from adjacent and all other signs. *Différance* incorporates this but it also indicates that the value of a sign is not immediately present; its value is **deferred** until the next sign in the syntagm "modifies" it.

Take the syntagm from the English song...

As we read from left to right, the "ten" gets transformed from "ten what?"...

...to the answer "ten green somethings".

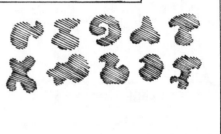

The question "ten green what?" is then modified to "ten green bottles".

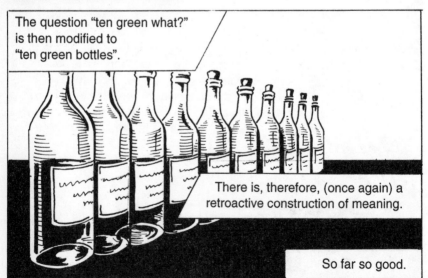

There is, therefore, (once again) a retroactive construction of meaning.

So far so good.

94

If we extend the syntagm to:

Ten green bottles standing on a wall

then further modifications take place. The ten items become items that are standing on the wall and the "answer" to "ten what?" is deferred again.

By the time that we get to "wall", having deferred our answer to what the bottles are standing on, we envisage the wall not as a bare one, but as one with ten bottles standing on it.

THE SIGN "WALL" THEREFORE BEARS THE TRACE OF PREVIOUS TERMS IN THE SYNTAGM (NAMELY "TEN GREEN BOTTLES")

DERRIDA

But think about this - does not the "ten green bottles", because of the process of deferral in *différance*, contain the **trace** of the "wall" which follows?

It is a bizarre proposition, given that "wall" is effectively a term from the future of that particular syntagm. But not so bizarre if meaning is constantly deferred until later.

Think also of the way in which "ten green bottles" also bears the trace of previous syntagms. Most people will anticipate that the song continues for some time with subsequent modifications.

Supposedly this was a unique syntagm, introduced only for the purpose of illustrating *différance*.

But no. It bears the traces of all the other renditions of this song, and all the future ones as well.

More troublesome than this is
the possibility that all texts are
traversed by the traces of other texts.

What does this mean?

The easiest way to think about this is to
imagine a text which is rich in allusion.

If we take any artefact of this kind, from
T. S. Eliot's difficult poem
The Waste Land (1922), to
Mel Brooks' spoof/tribute to Hitchcock,
High Anxiety (1978), it is clear that
enjoyment takes place on different levels.

It is eminently possible to enjoy both of
these texts without necessarily recognizing
all the references to past works that are in them.

But just because we don't register such
references doesn't mean they aren't there.

Undoubtedly, the phenomenon of *différance* encapsulates quite nicely the way in which we delude ourselves into thinking we are rational beings with a firm grip on the process of signification.

Différance, by its very nature, resists attempts to halt its flow.

Equally, what Lacan demonstrates about the subject as a "product" of signification, is irksome for those that believe in the rationality of humans acting independently outside of the signifying system, operating it in a voluntaristic way.

What post-structuralism does, then, is to up the stakes for semiotics. Signification becomes a powerful system in which human knowledge is wholly implicated.

In European intellectual circles after May '68, the works of Derrida and Lacan acted as important registers of the need to rethink signification and human agency.

Another important figure, Foucault, was less explicit in his orientation to semiotics.

NEVERTHELESS, I LOCATE THE POWER OF CERTAIN REGIMES (THE "HUMAN SCIENCES", PSYCHIATRY, CRIMINOLOGY, PSYCHOLOGY, ETC.) IN THE SIGNIFICATIONS THAT GIVE RISE TO DISCRETE **DISCOURSES.**

Such discourses set up the parameters for aspects of human subjectivity.

Post-structuralism is perhaps one of these constituting discourses, self-reflexively focussed on people and signification.

In Britain during the 1970s and early 1980s, both Foucault and Lacan became major intellectual figures (the latter especially in film theory and in bowdlerized form).

Derrida, on the other hand, was often resisted by the British academic establishment. Even in 1992, when he was probably the world's most famous philosopher, there was opposition to the offer of an honorary degree for him at Cambridge.

However, in the field of textual studies (mainly literary theory) Derrida became something of a guru through a series of professorships in the United States.

It was, perhaps, fitting that Derrida's exegetic principles should meet such a welcome in the United States.

Eagle-eyed readers will recognize that, through the notion of the interpretant and unlimited semiosis in particular, many of the arguments Derrida's sign theory has to make were implicit in the "semeiotic" of Charles Peirce.

American Semiotics

Numerous commentators argue that America has a long history of preoccupation with sign systems.

On the one hand there are the tracking skills of the Native American who lived on the ability to follow animals and interpret signs which would facilitate the animal's capture.

It is precisely this that is celebrated in one of the inaugural moments of American literature, the *Leatherstocking* novels of **James Fenimore Cooper** (1789-1851).

On the other hand there is the tradition of exegesis which is everywhere in the United States, from the Puritan readings of the Bible which forged New England in the 17th century, through the written Constitution, and up to the battles over political correctness in language which rage today.

These, in a sense, represent the split between "conventional" and "natural" signs. If semiosis is the ongoing flux of signification, then semiotics is the doctrine of signs.

What really sets American semiotics apart from European semiology is the former's roots in an attempt to address ALL kinds of sign interaction rather than just the human, conventional and cultural sign systems interrogated in structuralism and post-structuralism.

In its concern with the whole realm of semiosis, conventional and natural, American semiotics might be said to be made up of two broad fields of investigation - **anthroposemiotics** and **zoosemiotics**.

As such, its catholic embrace takes in much work which does not necessarily announce itself as explicitly "semiotic" in nature.

For example, the now commonplace study of "body language" as expounded by **David Efron** (b. 1904), or **Ray Birdwhistell** (b. 1918) in his "kinesics" (popularized - particularly in the 1970s - by the likes of Julius Fast).

Elsewhere, prominent thinkers have likewise operated with a semiotic remit: the sociologist **Erving Goffman** (1922-82), the communication theorist **Gregory Bateson** (1904-80), and the literary critic **Kenneth Burke** (1897-1993) among them.

The period between the death of Peirce and the preparation of his *Collected Papers* in 1931, however, is often felt to be an interregnum in American semiotics.

The most influential work in this period came from two English scholars, **C. K. Ogden** (1889-1957) and **I. A. Richards** (1893-1979), who published their opus *The Meaning of Meaning* in 1923. In spite of its acceptance in America and its lively exposition of Peirce in Appendix D, this did not forge an Anglo-American tradition of semiotic study.

Apart from the neglected work of **Victoria**, **Lady Welby** (1837-1912) - who is now known primarily as Peirce's correspondent - British semiotics remained buried in the work of philosophers in the tradition of **Bertrand Russell** (1872-1970) and **Ludwig Wittgenstein** (1889-1951).

Many of the major contributors to 20th century American semiotics were brilliant immigrants, although the first major thinker after Peirce was born on U.S. soil.

Charles Morris (1901-79) studied under **G. H. Mead** (1863-1931), who himself had studied under Peirce's friend and associate, **William James** (1842-1910).

Morris said of Peirce:

"His classification of signs, his refusal to separate completely animal and human sign-processes, his often penetrating remarks on linguistic categories, his application of semiotic to the problems of logic and philosophy, and the general acumen of his observations and distinctions, make his work in semiotic a source of stimulation that has few equals in the history of this field."

With *Foundation of the Theory of Signs* (1938) Morris began a major reorientation of semiotic study.

Morris conducted his initial work in a period when "behaviourism" dominated American thought. Drawing on the work of Russian physiologist **I. P. Pavlov** (1849-1936), many U.S. scholars considered human and animal behaviour in terms of responses to physical stimuli.

For a behaviourist linguist such as **Leonard Bloomfield** (1887-1949), language can be understood as a set of substitute responses to given stimuli. Moreover, these responses are observable in the light of human behaviour, not as the result of some theory of the relation between "thought" and "language".

Morris similarly conceived of semiosis as a chain of observable occurrences.

THIS CHAIN, WHICH MAKES UP "BEHAVIOUR" CONSISTS OF...

...ANY CHANGE TAKING PLACE IN AN ORGANISM WHICH HAS A BEGINNING AND A FINAL GOAL, THE LATTER OF WHICH IS DETERMINED BY AN IMPULSE.

Pavlov 1849-1936

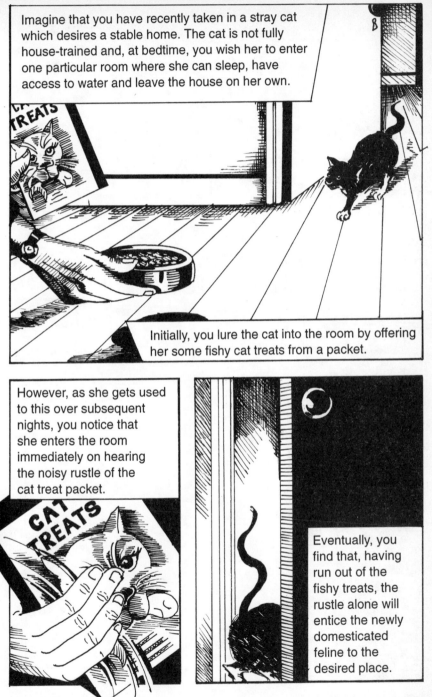

Imagine that you have recently taken in a stray cat which desires a stable home. The cat is not fully house-trained and, at bedtime, you wish her to enter one particular room where she can sleep, have access to water and leave the house on her own.

Initially, you lure the cat into the room by offering her some fishy cat treats from a packet.

However, as she gets used to this over subsequent nights, you notice that she enters the room immediately on hearing the noisy rustle of the cat treat packet.

Eventually, you find that, having run out of the fishy treats, the rustle alone will entice the newly domesticated feline to the desired place.

In terms of Morris' behaviourist semiotics, the original cat treat, accompanied by a rustling packet, sets up a disposition such that the rustle alone functions as a sign of the food.

The fact that the cat cannot eat the rustle - whereas it could eat the original cat treat - defines the rustle as very much a sign in the Peircean sense, standing in for an object.

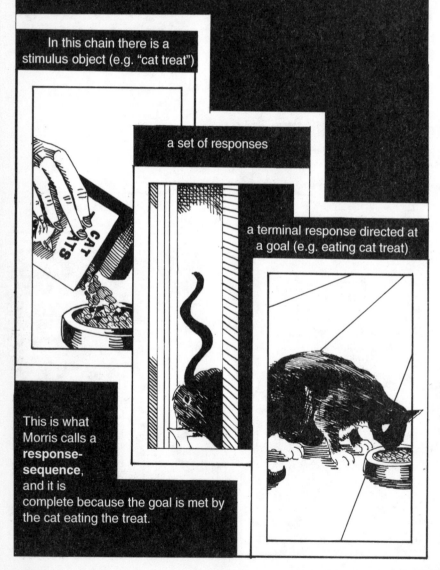

In this chain there is a stimulus object (e.g. "cat treat")

a set of responses

a terminal response directed at a goal (e.g. eating cat treat)

This is what Morris calls a **response-sequence**, and it is complete because the goal is met by the cat eating the treat.

Where the cat
cannot fulfil a
conventional goal
(e.g. cannot eat the rustle)
there is an incomplete
response-sequence.

It is within this frame that Morris
reworks Peirce's description of the sign.
For Morris, a response-sequence
consists of the following, as we see on
the next page.

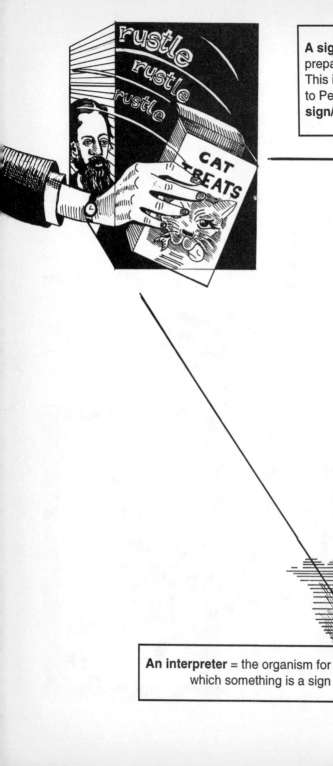

A sign =
preparatory stimulus.
This is analogous
to Peirce's
sign/representamen.

An interpreter = the organism for
which something is a sign

A Denotatum = Anything that would fulfil the disposition by permitting the completion of the response-sequence. This, then, is equivalent to Peirce's **object**.

A Significatum = The conditions for something to be a denotatum of the sign. This is not unlike Peirce's notion of the **ground**.

An Interpretant = disposition caused by a sign in the interpreter to participate in a response-sequence. This is equivalent to Peirce's term, especially as it is the third item which brings together the **representamen** and the **object**.

This schema provides the basis for Morris' understanding of the sign as "something that directs behaviour with respect to something that is not at the moment a stimulus".

But when these principles are extended into other areas of signification, Morris is vulnerable to the kind of criticisms lodged at behaviourism in general.

The alternative scenario of signification that Morris describes involves a lorry driver who takes a diversion from the prescribed route when informed of a landslide ahead.

DIVERSION

Clearly, the denotatum in Morris' schema should be the landslide itself. Similarly, the interpretant is the disposition to avoid the landslide set up by the informant's sign.

But can we be sure that this is so by simply observing landslide (denotatum), informant, sign, interpreter and final goal?

More specifically, is it the denotatum which activates the driver's response-sequence?

The presence (or promise) of food may cause a cat to respond in a certain way. However, when it comes to human motivations, complications set in.

It may be that the possibility of a successful diversion sets up the disposition to avoid the landslide. It may be that the strong desire to get to a destination on time dictates the avoidance of the landslide.

In each case, the landslide is not the denotatum, although it may be *observable* as such.

DIVERSION

Moreover, the unavailability of an alternative route would produce no response-sequence except that which could be observed as the driver stopping in the face of the blocked road.

It is possible that the behaviourism of Morris' semiotics precluded intellectual collaboration with other areas of American work in the field of signification.

While European explicators of sign systems have been influential in the formation of cultural, communication and media studies, the American forerunners of these disciplines have been found not in semiotics but in the related subjects of cybernetics, information and mass communication theory.

In the 1950s, theorists from different fields investigated the elements involved in message or signal transmission.

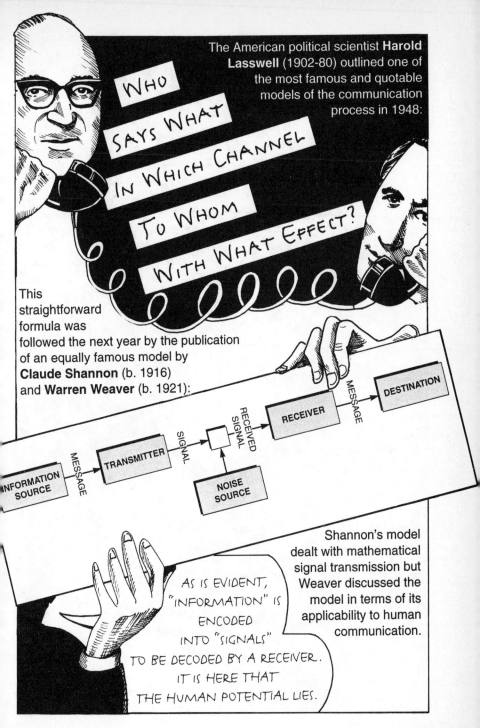

The American political scientist **Harold Lasswell** (1902-80) outlined one of the most famous and quotable models of the communication process in 1948:

WHO
SAYS WHAT
IN WHICH CHANNEL
TO WHOM
WITH WHAT EFFECT?

This straightforward formula was followed the next year by the publication of an equally famous model by **Claude Shannon** (b. 1916) and **Warren Weaver** (b. 1921):

INFORMATION SOURCE → MESSAGE → TRANSMITTER → SIGNAL → [NOISE SOURCE] → RECEIVED SIGNAL → RECEIVER → MESSAGE → DESTINATION

Shannon's model dealt with mathematical signal transmission but Weaver discussed the model in terms of its applicability to human communication.

AS IS EVIDENT, "INFORMATION" IS ENCODED INTO "SIGNALS" TO BE DECODED BY A RECEIVER. IT IS HERE THAT THE HUMAN POTENTIAL LIES.

The benefit of Shannon and Weaver's model was that it incorporated a degree of complexity into the information process. Encoding and decoding - rather than the straight flow of "pure" information from one source to a receiver - emphasized the subjectivity involved in communication, as did the "distortion" inherent in "Noise".

Additionally, communication models, like the semiotic work of Morris, were not fussy about the species of signification they sought to describe. All channels of communication were worthy of description within a given model's umbrella.

In fact, the early 1950s saw a wave of optimism regarding a unified theory of communication which would embrace elements of sociology, political science, semiotics, biology, linguistics, literary criticism and anthropology.

This was marked especially by a series of interdisciplinary conferences in New York and Chicago featuring the cyberneticist **Norbert Wiener** (1894-1964), the anthropologist **Margaret Mead** (1901-78), the sociologist **Talcott Parsons** (1902-79), the literary critic **I. A. Richards**, communication theorist **Gregory Bateson**, and others.

SEMIOSIS

But communication models - especially those developed in the wake of Shannon and Weaver - simply did not incorporate the flexibility in their linear schema to deal with the vicissitudes of semiosis.

Confronting the complexity of semiosis, Morris had divided semiotics into three discrete areas.

The first dealt with the relations between a sign and other signs (i.e. relations of combination) which he called **syntactics**.

The second concerned relations between signs and denotata (i.e. relations of denotating) which he called **semantics**.

The third comprised relations between signs and interpreters (i.e. relations of emphasis) which he called **pragmatics**.

Morris *Lips*

Eye *Diamonds*

These areas are not dissimilar from those which are designated by the same terms in contemporary linguistics.

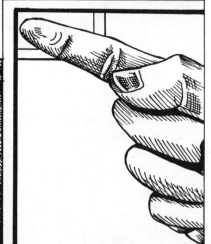

I INTENDED THE THREEFOLD DISTINCTION TO TRAVERSE MORE THAN THE FIELD OF ANTHROPOSEMIOSIS.

Morris' student, a polymath called **Thomas Sebeok** (b.1920), a participant in the 1950s conferences, was subsequently the major force in international semiotics.

MY WORK WAS TO TRANSCEND THE STALEMATE OF BEHAVIOURISM AND FRUITFULLY LEAD SEMIOTICS BEYOND THE BOUNDS OF MERELY HUMAN PHENOMENA.

Born in Budapest in 1920...

...Sebeok travelled to the United States in 1937 where he attended the University of Chicago, thereafter pursuing graduate studies as a linguist at Princeton.

Sebeok is therefore one of the many immigrants who make up the chimera known as "American semiotics", along with philosophers such as **Ernst Cassirer** (1874-1945) from Germany, **Rudolf Carnap** (1891-1970) from Austria, **Jacques Maritain** (1882-1973) from France and the linguist **Roman Jakobson** (1896-1982), from Russia.

119

Since 1943, Sebeok has taught at Indiana University in Bloomington, and it is from this base that he has tirelessly agitated on behalf of semiotics, editing numerous series of new titles and neglected masterpieces, founding the International Association for Semiotic Studies (IASS) in 1969 and, from the same date, acting as editor-in-chief for the eclectic international journal *Semiotica*.

It is largely by dint of this administrative profile set up by Sebeok that the term "semiotics" has superseded "semiology" on both sides of the Atlantic.

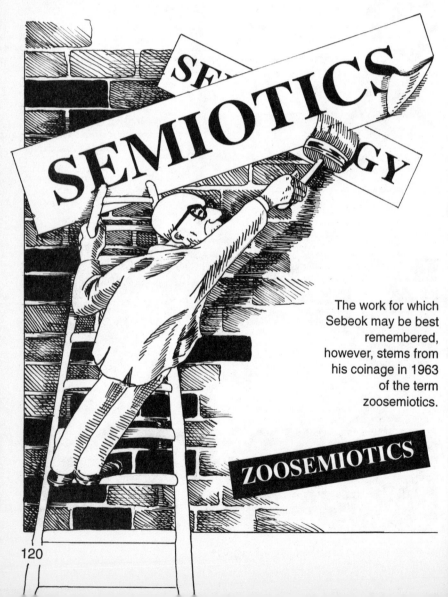

The work for which Sebeok may be best remembered, however, stems from his coinage in 1963 of the term zoosemiotics.

Sebeok's linguistic training, far from confining him to the study of human communication, provided the impetus for non-linguistic study and a scrutiny of the animal realm.

A MUTUAL APPRECIATION OF GENETICS, ANIMAL COMMUNICATION STUDIES, AND LINGUISTICS, MAY LEAD TO A FULL UNDERSTANDING OF THE DYNAMICS OF SEMIOSIS, AND THIS MAY, IN THE LAST ANALYSIS, TURN OUT TO BE NO LESS THAN THE DEFINITION OF LIFE.

I DEFINE MYSELF AS A BIOLOGIST 'MANQUÉ' AS WELL AS, CONCURRENTLY, A DOCTRINAIRE OF SIGNS 'MALGRÉ LUI.'

However, signification is not conceived by him as something that directs behaviour in the way that Morris had envisaged.

121

For Sebeok, one of the chief defining characteristics of the "zoosemiotic" is that, unlike the "anthroposemiotic", it is without a language.

Many studies have been devoted to animal communication, especially in the post-war period, but these have often falsely posited an animal "language".

Probably the most famous study of animal signs is that of the Nobel Prize winner, **Karl von Frisch** (1886-1982), who, in the 1920s, observed the "dances" of bees.

Similarly, there have been studies of the diversity of birdsongs which are often found to be distinguished by regional dialects and certainly depend on learning.

On a slightly different level, some gorillas in captivity have been observed to have acquired as many as 224 words in a special sign language.

But, as regards the question of whether animals possess a language, Sebeok steadfastly says "No!"

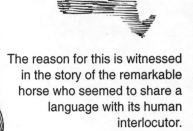

The reason for this is witnessed in the story of the remarkable horse who seemed to share a language with its human interlocutor.

NO!

In numerous such cases of an animal responding to human attempts at communication - for example, doing sums by stamping a hoof repeatedly - it can be shown that the animal is not responding to the manifest human signs.

Instead, it feeds off the various non-verbal cues of the interlocutor, which have often been deliberately introduced in the service of a hoax.

Sebeok calls this kind of misconstruing of animal communication "the Clever Hans Effect", after the most celebrated case of its kind.

However, the phenomenon is not just important for its use in the sceptical debunking of (un)intentional hoaxes.

WHAT'S 2 + 2?

TOK
TOK
TOK
TOK

The interesting feature of the Clever Hans Effect is that for spectators - and some human participants in such exercises - the signs that the humans receive back from the animal are **not animal in origin**.

Effectively, the signs emanate from the human who provides the cues in the first place. The sender thus receives his/her own message back from the receiver in distorted form.

Drawing on the work of the Estonian-born German biologist, **Jakob von Uexküll** (1864-1944), Sebeok describes how semiosis takes place in a significant environment or *Umwelt*.

All semiosis, for Sebeok, occurs within two universal sign systems: the **genetic** and **verbal** codes.

The genetic code (found in all organisms on the planet by way of DNA and RNA), and the verbal code of all peoples (the underlying structure which makes all languages possible).

Within this are the mutually-serving organism and its *Umwelt* (or significant environment).

The *Umwelt* is the part of an environment that an organism "chooses" to inhabit; it is the perceptual or "subjective" universe of the organism.

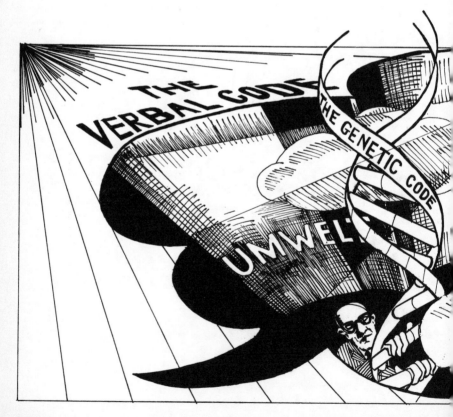

But the organism also acts as a sign of the *Umwelt* in that the structure of the organism will, in some sense, give clues to the nature of its environment.

Conversely, the *Umwelt* also shows that it is itself a sign of the organism, in that it is possible to make inferences about the organism based on an analysis of its environment.

Umwelt and organism are brought together - in a quasi-Peircean way - by a third factor, in the form of a code that Sebeok, following Uexküll, calls a "meaning-plan".

This code is a master entity, in that it is outside the organism proper and precedes the organism's existence.

Yet the organism enacts an ongoing process of interpreting its *Umwelt*; it gives birth to new organisms, which are born into a pre-existing *Umwelt* but which contribute to a further interpretation or chain of the ongoing *Umwelt*.

This is a very comprehensive conception of semiosis: it is one that takes in many sources and, like the communication theory of the 1950s, envisages many possible channels.

When Sebeok considers sources, it becomes clear how human signification - anthroposemiosis - is only a small part of a universe of signs.

If this was not diverse enough, consider Sebeok's classification of the channels through which senders and receivers of messages can interact:

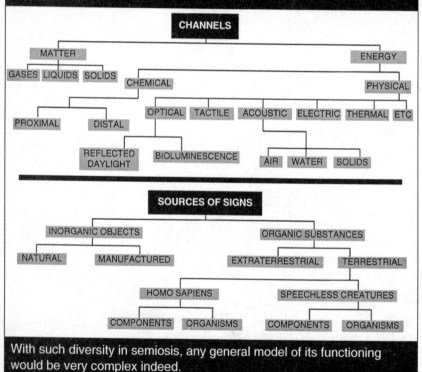

With such diversity in semiosis, any general model of its functioning would be very complex indeed.

What Sebeok's work allows is a wider understanding of semiosis and its modelling processes. It also allows for a reassessment of whole semiotic traditions.

Soviet Semiotics

In 1970, Sebeok found himself in Estonia where he was the subject of an impromptu invitation to address the fourth biennial Tartu Summer School on Semiotics.

Given the centrality of *Umwelt* to his work, it was appropriate that Sebeok should broach the related topic of "modelling" or, to put it another way, "a programme of behaviour". "Modelling" implies a conception of the world "where the environment stands in reciprocal relationship with some other system, such as an individual organism, a collectivity, a computer, or the like, and where its reflection functions as a control of this system's total mode of communication".

In this formulation, the products of human behaviour - linguistic texts, cultures, social institutions - are not so much the result of an unfathomable creativity as of a series of limitations or choices of operation.

Sebeok's chosen topic was also appropriate because Soviet semiotics is well-known for its work with the notion of "modelling", a hypothesis whose central tenets have had a troubled but fecund history in Russian intellectual life.

Soviet semiotics evolved from some key strands in 20th century Russian thought.

At the turn of the century, materialists such as **G.V. Plekhanov** (1856-1918) and Marxists such as **V.I. Lenin** (1870-1924) had included theories of signs and consciousness in their philosophical writings, as had those intellectuals who are referred to as "neo-Kantians".

But probably the most important moment for Russian semiotics came in the years immediately preceding the Russian Revolution in 1917.

Sergej Karcevskij (1894-1955), a student who had attended Saussure's course in Geneva, returned to Moscow in 1917 and brought with him a repository of ideas which fell on the fertile minds of the Moscow Linguistic Circle (1915-21).

Headed by the young Roman Jakobson - who also wrote poetry under the name Aljagrov - the Circle had links with another organization.

MOSCOW LINGUISTIC

The Petrograd Society for the Study of Poetic Language (or OPOJAZ, 1916-30), was the hub of Russian Formalism and featured the participation of, among others, **Boris Ejxenbaum** (1886-1959), **Viktor Sklovskij** (1893-1985), **Jurij Tynyanov** (1894-1943), **Petr Bogatyrev** (1893-1971) and, again, Roman Jakobson.

It is difficult to provide a watertight definition of Russian Formalism; indeed, the name itself was bestowed upon the group by its opponents.

While the work of the Petrograd group did not consist of an exclusive concern with "form" as the name "formalist" (with a small "f") might suggest, it did explore the specific *character* of literature.

These theorists developed an understanding of the literary text which focused on its very literariness *(literaturnost)* and its capacity of "making strange'" *(ostranenie)*, both demarcating it as **specifically** a literary entity.

Likewise, the Moscow Circle started to examine the notion of the peculiarly **aesthetic function** which gave poetic language its seemingly intrinsic nature.

O.P.O.J.A

CERTAIN COMMUNICATIONS MAY CONTAIN MANY ELEMENTS WHICH MAKE THEM COMPLEX, MULTILAYERED STRUCTURES, BUT THEY CAN ALSO CONTAIN A SPECIAL COMPONENT WHICH IMPUTES AN OVERALL CHARACTER TO THE COMMUNICATION.

In the case of "artistic" texts, this is a dominating "aesthetic" component. Artistic texts such as poems may have a referential component which allows them to make reference to the world; but a poem is not straightforwardly a document of cultural history, social relations or biography. Instead, it has an aesthetic aspect which might be termed its "poeticity", that use of language which makes it a poem and not prose.

These were ideas that Jakobson took with him when he left Russia for Prague in 1920. However, he maintained links with his old Formalist colleagues and, in 1928, published with Tynyanov eight theses under the title "Problems in the Study of Language and Literature".

Here, Jakobson and Tynyanov elaborated their own notion of what constitutes a "structure". Where "structuralists" such as Lévi-Strauss hold that all cultural artefacts are organized "grammatically", like a language, Jakobson and Tynyanov insisted that "structures" contained their own laws rather than just linguistic ones.

Systems, then, were viewed as relational and dynamic; the work of "art" might be autonomous, but it was not a structure closed off from the world.

In a sense, this negated much of the work done by the Formalists, for whom literature - while it was certainly an autonomous structure of literariness *(literaturnost)* - was not to be understood for its referential possibilities or its sociological contents, both of which it might have in common with other structures.

The work of "art" in Jakobson and Tynyanov's theses was far from being unique in its structural composition. It consisted of a system and structure like any other semiotic entity, the difference being that the "aesthetic" component of its system was dominant.

For the Stalinist regime, which gained ascendancy in the 1930s, such contentions might prove threatening to a theory of "art" predicated on the uplifting aspirations of "Socialist Realism".

There can be little coincidence, then, that a Soviet semiotics not too distantly related to the 1920s tradition of work on structures could only emerge in the post-Stalin period, from the late 1950s on.

Jurij Lotman (1922-93), the leading figure in the Renaissance of semiotics in the Soviet Union, was originally a professor of literature specializing in works surrounding the "Decembrist" revolt against Tsarism in 1822.

BUT MY WORK ON LITERARY THEORY BECAME CHARACTERIZED BY THE USE OF SUCH TERMS AS "LANGUAGE", "CODE", "ENTROPY", "NOISE" ETC.

Like his colleagues in Moscow, **V. V. Ivanov, I. I. Revzin** and **Boris Uspenskij** (who had founded the Association for Machine Translation in 1955), Lotman was now addressing culture in terms of the characteristic ways in which it transfers and processes items of information. As such, he was applying **information theory** - from the early development of computers - to the most cherished of sign systems.

7.

Here, once more, was an assault on the whole edifice of "Literature", an assault that might be called "anti-humanist" precisely because it bracketed the supposed "spiritual", "human", "ennobling" qualities of an artefact in favour of scrutinizing its informational bearing.

Claude Shannon had devised his groundbreaking communication model in order to present in "digital" form all the bits that went into making the "analogue" product. In one sense, this kind of procedure constitutes quite a radical attack on traditional modes of thinking.

We can visualize time as a clockface. Each space between the numbers analogically represents something.

Digital representation is different. A digital watch simply tells you the time in numbers; there is no space on a digital watch which is analogous to "five minutes".

An analogue which seems to be all of a piece (e.g. a lecture to an audience, a painting in a gallery, etc.) could be shown in digital form (e.g. as *Information Source, Transmitter, Signal,* etc.)

The digital approach is, essentially, the *modus operandi* of Lévi-Strauss in his analysis of the Oedipus myth (see page 62). This is also what the Soviet semioticians proceeded to do in the 1960s. In a series of Summer Schools at Tartu State University beginning in 1964, Jurij Lotman outlined a theory of culture.

CULTURE IS
THE TOTALITY OF
NON-HEREDITARY INFORMATION ACQUIRED,
PRESERVED AND TRANSMITTED BY THE
VARIOUS GROUPS OF HUMAN SOCIETY.

The heartless assault on humanist logic that this may at first seem is dispelled when one considers that all cultures *are* characterized by a repository of knowledge which is passed on to current and new members of that culture.

But culture is not just a store. For the Soviet semioticians of the 60s and 70s, culture is also a "Secondary Modelling System": it provides an ongoing model for human knowledge and interaction.

The "*Primary* Modelling System" is the language capacity which is considered to be a natural system in relation to all others and is referred to as "natural language".

NOTE *The merging of information theory and semiotics of culture by Lotman represents an amazing prescience of the underlying theory of cyberspace.*

Because culture is built on natural language, Lotman suggests that one way culture might be classified is in its conceptualization of the sign.

The examples he takes are the cultures of the (Russian) Middle Ages and the Enlightenment.

137

The Middle Ages are characterized by semiotic abundance. Every object has the potential of semiosis and meaning is everywhere. Nothing is insignificant.

The Enlightenment, on the other hand, is characterized by a belief in reason and the rational eschewing of all artifice. The "natural" is valued over the "cultural" (i.e. "unnatural" or artificial - as embodied in the constructions known as signs).

In fact, there is a hierarchy of signification, starting with the lowly object and ascending to those things which most successfully signify nobility, power, holiness and wisdom.

In one way, Saussure embodies a high point of such rationality by way of his belief in the "unnatural", "arbitrary" nature of the linguistic sign.

For Lotman, then, semiotics represents not just a scientific method; it also constitutes late 20th century consciousness.

Yet it should not be forgotten, as V. V. Ivanov states, that "possession of natural language and the sign systems constructed upon it is the specific particularity of man".

In the essay "In What Sense is Language a 'Primary Modelling System'?"(1988) Sebeok clarifies the status of "language" in relation to the history of humans and semiosis.

Only in the genus *homo* have verbal signs emerged; apes, for example, simply cannot speak. But hominids have more than just the **anthroposemiotic verbal**; they also possess the **zoosemiotic non-verbal**. As Sebeok points out,

Evolutionists have traced the expanding brain size of early humans, through *Homo habilis* and *Homo erectus* to *Homo sapiens sapiens.* The range of activities and tools that each utilized suggests that they also possessed the capacity for differentiation and, concomitantly, language.

SOVIET SCHOLARS CALL THE FORMER "PRIMARY" BUT, IN FACT, IT IS SECONDARY.

The minds of early humans, it appears, were sufficiently developed to be able to process different kinds of information. They could, in their mental operations, harbour distinct fragments of information, each of which was placed in discrete compartments in the manner described by some theories of language.

BUT EARLY HUMANS DID NOT SPEAK TO EACH OTHER

There was a developed capacity for language; but this was unaccompanied by speech. Language therefore evolved for the purposes of cognitive modelling rather than the purposes of communicative message-swapping. As such, language can be understood as mental processing rather than as a tool for communicating with other beings.

THE PRIMARY MODELLING SYSTEM IN SEMIOTICS IS, MORE ACCURATELY, THE NON-VERBAL MODELLING OF ALL ORGANISMS IN TANDEM WITH THEIR "UMWELT"

Communication among early humans was carried out by non-verbal means; it was only later that language was co-opted for the verbal communicative function.

Nevertheless, the bulk of study in semiotics, especially in Europe, focuses upon humans and their relation to communication artefacts (i.e. the relation of language/speech to culture or the relation of "secondary" modelling systems to "tertiary" ones).

Much of the important contemporary work on readers and texts in semiotics is derived from the *oeuvres* of theorists that bridge disparate traditions.

Roman Jakobson, the Prague School and Beyond

A student of the Russian phonologist **Nikolai Troubetzkoy** (1890-1939), Jakobson has been a major influence on 20th century semiotics, as his numerous appearances in these pages testify.

Umberto Eco puts it like this: "Let me assume that the reason Jakobson never wrote a book on semiotics is that his entire scientific existence was a living example of a Quest for Semiotics."

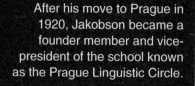

After his move to Prague in 1920, Jakobson became a founder member and vice-president of the school known as the Prague Linguistic Circle.

The Circle - which included **Vilém Mathesius** (1882-1945), **Jan Mukařovský** (1891-1975) and Jakobson's long-time colleague, Petr Bogatyrev - met from 1926 to 1948.

Crucial to the semiotics of Jakobson and the others was a notion of "structure" as evolutionary and not hermetically sealed.

Language, according to the German philosopher **Wilhelm von Humboldt** (1767-1835), should be conceived as a process *(energia)* rather than as a final product *(ergon)*.

This had a significant influence on the Prague School, as did the Jakobson/Tynyanov theses of 1928 which insisted that systems need to be studied as changeable entities:

LANGU

LANGUA

LANGUA

LANGUA

LANGUA

LANGUAG

LANGUAG

LANGUAG

LANGUAG

LANGUAGE

LANGUAGE

LANGUAGE

"Pure synchrony now proves to be an illusion . . . The opposition between synchrony and diachrony was an opposition between the concept of system and the concept of evolution; thus it loses its importance in principle as soon as we recognize that every system necessarily exists as an evolution, whereas, on the other hand, evolution is inescapably of a systemic nature."

Jakobson's work remained steadfastly committed to an understanding of signification as consisting of **complex** and **overlapping** structures.

In 1939, when the Nazis invaded Czechoslovakia, Jakobson moved to Scandinavia where he was visiting lecturer at the universities of Copenhagen, Oslo and Uppsala. In 1941 he moved to the United States, where he stayed as an academic and became the leading post-war figure in American semiotics.

His work bridged traditions ranging from his early Saussurean leanings and the "structuralism" of the Prague School to information theory and his discovery of Peirce.

Take Saussure's notion of the "arbitrariness" of the linguistic sign. In Peirce's terms one could say that this kind of sign is a **symbol**. But, as Jakobson shows, it can be an **icon** and an **index**.
Let's have an example.....

ARBITRARY

VENI, VIDI, VICI.

A SYMBOL

AN ICON AND AN INDEX

Julius Caesar's words "*Veni, vidi, vici*" ("I came, I saw, I conquered") are resonant, perhaps, because they **iconically** represent the series of events they describe.

The statement "The president and secretary of state attended the meeting" contains this sequence because it iconically indicates ranking importance.

More importantly, the linguistic sign can be an **index** because it is in a relation of causation with its speaker. Borrowing from the linguist **Otto Jespersen** (1860-1943), Jakobson calls **indices** of this kind "shifters".

These items - also known as **deictic** categories - point to the cause and context of an utterance.

As Benveniste notes, every time "I" is uttered it is different because we have to know who is using "I" to comprehend the utterance which contains it.

This is the property of the shifter - it shifts emphasis onto the situation of the utterance. Think of all the lexical items that do this:

Personal pronouns

I

YOU

HE/SHE

WE US

THEM

Indicators of place **Indicators of time** **Indicators of specificity**

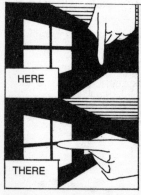

HERE

THERE

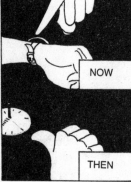

NOW

THEN

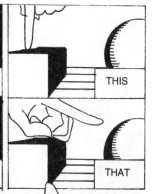

THIS

THAT

And so on.

All of these require knowledge of the situation of utterance; all of them are therefore **context-sensitive**.

But, perhaps above all, they embody what Jakobson calls the **referential function**.

That is to say, they are likely to appear in a communication whose main purpose is to make reference to something in the world.

In what is probably his most famous essay, Jakobson develops this very Prague-style understanding of signification by merging it with information theory to construct a general model of the communication event.

Substituting *langue* and *parole* for **code** and **message**, he outlines the features of any communication:

CONTEXT

ADDRESSER   MESSAGE   ADDRESSEE

CONTACT

CODE

Onto this map of features he superimposes corresponding **functions**:

referential

emotive   poetic   conative

phatic

metalingual

Thus, the **emotive** function dominates in a communication when there is a focus on the ADDRESSER, e.g. interjections such as "Tut! Tut!" which express an addresser's dismay and are primarily self-serving.

NO SMOKING

The **conative** function (not to be confused with connotative) dominates when there is focus on the ADDRESSEE, e.g. commands such as "Stop!"

The **phatic** function dominates when there is emphasis on the CONTACT, usually to establish or maintain communication, e.g. "Lend me your ears" or "Are you listening?"

The **metalingual** function dominates when there is focus on the CODE, e.g. to check if it's working: "Do you know what I mean?"

As we have seen, the **referential** function really comes into play when there is a focus on the CONTEXT (markedly so when shifters are present).

And the **poetic** function dominates when there is a focus on the MESSAGE, e.g. the campaign slogan "I like Ike" is a political communication, but its chief feature is that it is succinct and "poetically" makes "liking" and Eisenhower synonymous.

In fact, this is the value of Jakobson's model: it is flexible, demonstrating how communications can have distinct layers that may be dominant on occasions.

The dominant function may change with the situation, even though its components remain the same. For instance, our **metalingual** example - "Do you know what I mean?" - has been used so often by the British boxer and well-loved celebrity, Frank Bruno, that it has now become a catch-phrase used in a **phatic** mode to maintain communication.

KNOW WHAT I MEAN?

Jakobson's model has far-reaching consequences for semiotics, both in its consideration of ADDRESSEE **and** ADDRESSER and in its vision of communication as the product of a structuring hierarchy of functions.

Jan Mukařovský's work on the **aesthetic function** has related imperatives, and is similarly important.

I SEE THE AESTHETIC FUNCTION AS PERMEATING THE DIVERSITY OF COLLECTIVE LIFE: IN BUILDINGS, IN BODILY ADORNMENT (FASHION), IN DESIGN OF HOUSEHOLD OBJECTS ETC.

Conversely, he sees, like Jakobson, that such a function might dominate in "aesthetic" objects but that it might not be the only function in operation.

In "Literature", for example, there is also a **communicative function** at play.

In the Prague tradition, Mukařovský insists that the aesthetic function is not at all divorced from other areas of life, although in the object presumed to be "aesthetic" it structures that which is within its domain. The function can be separated into **norms** and **values**.

An **aesthetic norm** arises from interaction with other norms in a social formation. It structures what is and isn't held to be "aesthetic".

Aesthetic value, which is usually harboured by individuals, is stabilized by the norm. Moreover, it is sustained by institutions:

"Society creates the institutions and organs with which it influences aesthetic value through regulation or evaluation of art works. Among those institutions are art criticism, expertise, artistic training (including art schools and institutions whose goal is the cultivation of passive contemplation), the marketing of art works and its advertising, surveys to determine the most valuable work of art, art shows, museums, public libraries, competitions, prizes, academies and, frequently, censorship."

This is an incredibly modern understanding of "art" when one considers that Mukařovský was writing at a time - 1936 - when mass culture theorists in the West and Soviet ideologues in the East were refusing to contemplate "art" as anything other than an intrinsically lofty and spiritual entity.

Most importantly for Mukařovský, the work of "art" is a sign and therefore a social fact. As a sign, it has a potential communicative function, it stands in for something and - as Jakobson insists - it emanates from an ADDRESSER to an ADDRESSEE.

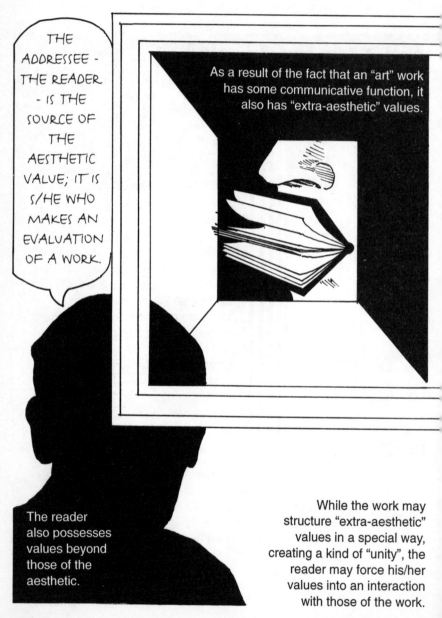

THE ADDRESSEE - THE READER - IS THE SOURCE OF THE AESTHETIC VALUE; IT IS S/HE WHO MAKES AN EVALUATION OF A WORK.

As a result of the fact that an "art" work has some communicative function, it also has "extra-aesthetic" values.

The reader also possesses values beyond those of the aesthetic.

While the work may structure "extra-aesthetic" values in a special way, creating a kind of "unity", the reader may force his/her values into an interaction with those of the work.

Mukařovský did not speculate too far about what happens when this kind of interaction takes place. However, his Prague disciple, **Felix Vodicka** (1909-74), did initiate such a task, calling for focus on:-

- **how the work is perceived;**
- **what values are ascribed to it;**
- **in which form it appears to those who experience it aesthetically;**
- **what semantic connections it evokes;**
- **in what social milieu it exists;**
- **in what hierarchical order.**

For Vodicka, the chief component of the reader's semiotic interaction with a text consisted of what the Polish philosopher **Roman Ingarden** (1893-1970) called "concretization".

A "concretization" is a reader's actualization of a text. In a sentence such as "The man stood in the corner", a reader will actualize the text by contributing a sense of the man's age, size, skin colour, clothing, facial appearance, emotions, etc., as well as the nature of the corner in question and the exact way he stood.

For Vodicka, concretizations are not simply dictated by the work. The work as sign - as Mukařovský insisted - is social in nature and evokes norms and values for the reader who also carries a range of "extra-aesthetic" values.

Concretization therefore takes place on the grounds of readers' social imperatives, what they bring to texts as a result of their participation in the complex interaction of aesthetic values and norms and extra-aesthetic ones.

In its stress on the social context, the work of Jakobson and the Prague School is extremely important. It prefigures many contemporary concerns in semiotics, such as:

- the multilayered structures of semiosis
- the relation of (aesthetic) texts to institutionally sustained norms and values
- the relation of (aesthetic) texts to values beyond the aesthetic realm
- the role of context in the meaning of texts
- the role of the reader in actualizing texts

In media, communications and cultural studies alone since the 1980s there has likewise been an overwhelming concern with the reader and the reading process.

One leading semiotician who, like Jakobson, bridges disparate traditions, has contributed a great deal to debates on these issues.

Limiting Semiosis

Umberto Eco (b. 1932) is a medieval historian, an essayist, a novelist, but, perhaps above all, a semiotician.

His work contains a productive synthesis of virtually all the 20th century schools of semiotics, supported by a vast knowledge of the classical heritage of sign study.

In spite of Eco's avoidance of scholasticism, he has not been overwhelmed by a semiotic glut.

In his popular essay, "Fragments" (1959), a post-apocalyptic Arctic civilization uncovers and interprets artefacts from the regions to the south:

"We have here a line - alas, the only legible one - of what must have been an ode condemning terrestrial concerns: 'It's a material world.' Immediately after that we are struck by the lines of another fragment, apparently from a propitiatory or fertility hymn to nature: 'I'm singing in the rain, just singing in the rain, it's a glorious feeling . . .' It is easy to imagine this sung by a chorus of young girls: the delicate words evoke the image of maidens in white veils dancing at sowing time in some *pervigilium*."

Clearly, the Arctic civilization, with too little evidence to hand, embark on a project of gauche over-interpretation.

Eco warns of this danger throughout his career.

At about the same time that he wrote "Fragments", Eco was also writing, under the influence of information theory, about his conception of the "open work".

At first glance this formulation seems like one more attempt to demarcate "high" from "low" culture. As it identifies "open" with "modern" and "closed" with "popular" it also seems to resemble similar formulations made elsewhere since the 1960s in France (Barthes' writerly/readerly), in Britain (Colin MacCabe's "Classic realist text"/revolutionary text) and in Germany (by Wolfgang Iser).

But Eco's formulation is slightly different.

> THE "OPEN WORK" IS A TEXT WHICH HAILS A PARTICULAR KIND OF READER, DISTINCT FROM THAT OF THE "CLOSED WORK" WHICH OFTEN PRESUPPOSES AN "AVERAGE" READER.

The "closed" text allows a myriad of possible interpretations at each point, although it is ruled by a fairly rigid logic which looks like this:

The ADDRESSER (not the author but the structure of the text) offers the ADDRESSEE occasions to make up his/her own mind, yet ultimately forecloses these (an example might be the clues/red herrings which eventually lead to the denouement of a detective novel).

The "open" text, on the other hand, entails a "Model Reader" - one can extrapolate a good *Ulysses* reader from the text itself - and can be envisaged as:

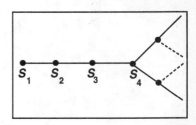

The ADDRESSER here leads the ADDRESSEE and then allows him/her to make up his/her own mind and (re)assess the previous moves from this vantage point.

What happens, for Eco, in the reading of a text is not unlike the process of "concretization". The reader goes through a series of motions to decode the signs.

BUT, IN THIS DECODING, THERE IS THE POSSIBILITY OF - IN PEIRCE'S TERMS - "UNLIMITED SEMIOSIS" AS EACH SIGN GIVES WAY TO A CONNECTED ONE AND SO ON, POTENTIALLY AD INFINITUM.

How, then, is it possible to make such semiosis purposeful? How is it possible to interpret a text without following the overconfident predictions of the Arctic civilization? Is it the case that a text has as many meanings as there are readers?

Eco addresses these questions by comparing Peirce with Hermetism (alchemy or occult science) in the Renaissance. The latter held that every symbol was related to like symbol, continuously.

For example, some Hermetists thought that the plant orchis had some form of human testicles (from the Greek *orkhis* = testicles). Therefore, every operation undertaken on the plant which gets a result would also get one if undertaken on the human.

This could have been painful. However, the "testicles" of the *orchis* and those of the human developed for totally different reasons. They are genetically distinct, even if they seem similar.

A **Habit**, according to Peirce, is "that which determines us, from given premisses, to draw one inference rather than another", and is "constitutional or acquired".

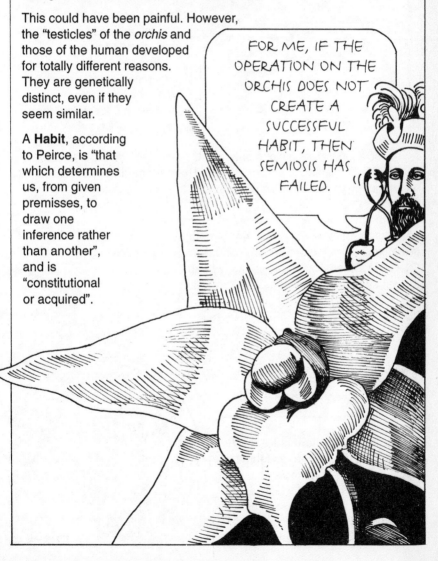

FOR ME, IF THE OPERATION ON THE ORCHIS DOES NOT CREATE A SUCCESSFUL HABIT, THEN SEMIOSIS HAS FAILED.

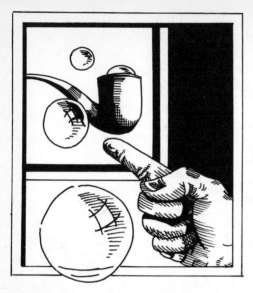

As we have seen, a **Habit** is associated with the **Interpretant** which, itself, is part of the realm of *Thirdness* or reasoning. Unlike Derridean *différance*, Peircean unlimited semiosis takes place with the ultimate goal of getting to what the sign **stands for**.

As Eco points out, semiosis may mean the movement from one interpretant to another, but for Peirce there lies a **purpose** behind this.

An association between signs does not take place on an arbitrary or chaotic basis; instead it is guided by the **Habitual** means by which we - as a community of humans - draw inferences.

The sign involves a Representamen, by means of an Interpretant engendering an **Immediate Object** (the object as represented). We can never grasp the real, **Dynamic Object**, but it has certainly been the cause of the Immediate Object.

THE QUEST THAT UNLIMITED SEMIOSIS ENACTS IS DIRECTED AT THE GOAL OF A FINAL INTERPRETANT.

This **Final Interpretant** is also the **Habit**, a disposition (as Morris would say) to act on the world. And it is semiosis itself which builds up the world by means of the relation of the Immediate and Final Interpretants.

The real (object) is what information and reasoning would finally result in. That is to say that the real is actually the **intersubjective** meaning arrived at by a **community** in semiosis.

One way to think of this community might be the notion of a research hothouse of semiosis.

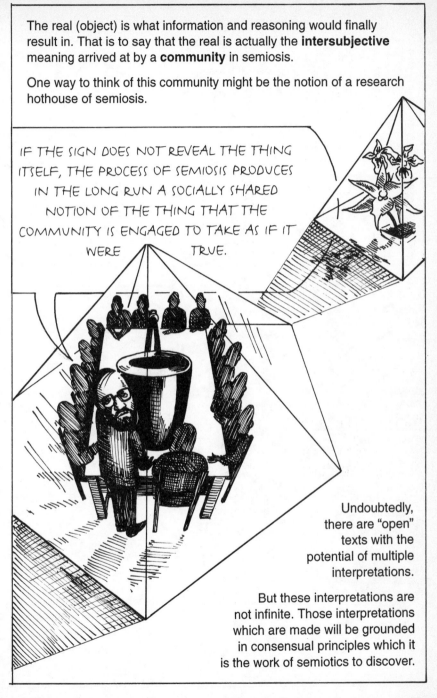

IF THE SIGN DOES NOT REVEAL THE THING ITSELF, THE PROCESS OF SEMIOSIS PRODUCES IN THE LONG RUN A SOCIALLY SHARED NOTION OF THE THING THAT THE COMMUNITY IS ENGAGED TO TAKE AS IF IT WERE TRUE.

Undoubtedly, there are "open" texts with the potential of multiple interpretations.

But these interpretations are not infinite. Those interpretations which are made will be grounded in consensual principles which it is the work of semiotics to discover.

161

For Eco, a serious semiotics should be concerned to weed out bad interpretations in order to establish the principles of those which arise from successful semiosis, alighting ultimately, perhaps, on a Final Interpretant.

Maybe, when we have used semiotics with sufficient acumen, it can become a predictive tool.

The Present

The Saussurean tradition of semiology has, largely, embodied what might be called a "nominalist" outlook. It holds that we cannot really get at the world of the real because all that comes to us is totally mediated by signs.

Jean Baudrillard (b.1929) as a thinker is constituted by the nominalist tradition.

SUCH SEEMINGLY REAL ENTITIES AS HUMAN NEED, MARX'S "USE-VALUE" AND EVEN THE SUN, ARE SIMPLY "ALIBIS" OF RELATIONS OF PURE EXCHANGE.

THIS EXCHANGE IS NOT UNLIKE THE DIFFERENCE ENVISAGED BY ME AS THE ROOT OF "VALUE".

MY TRADITION OF SEMIOTICS, ON THE OTHER HAND, IS MAINLY A "REALIST" ONE.

Thinkers such as Eco and Sebeok are confident of the ability to apprehend the "real", although it is an arduous process and involves a continuous reformulation, beyond a simple belief in objective concrete entities, of what the "real" actually is.

As we have seen, the Soviet theorist Lotman believes the present to be distinguished by a semiotic consciousness.

IT IS THE TASK OF FUTURE SEMIOTICIANS TO IMPLEMENT PEIRCEAN SEMIOTICS, SAUSSUREAN SEMIOLOGY, OR A SYNTHESIS OF BOTH TO INTERPRET THE WORLD.

However, it would be remiss to end this book without briefly demonstrating that the act of semiotic analysis is actually an act of *agency*, potentially changing or contributing to the world of semiosis.

Two examples will suffice.

Interestingly, they are taken from Britain, a country which has hitherto featured little in this account of semiotics.

Social Semiotics

Deriving from the work of the British linguist, **M. A. K. Halliday** (b. 1925), "social semiotics" was developed by theorists in Britain and Australia whose background was often that of linguistics or literary study and who found themselves in university departments devoted to media and cultural studies.

Halliday does not envisage the split between *langue* and *parole* as absolute in the way that Saussure does. Rather, like Vološinov, who had criticized Saussure in the late 1920s for focusing on *langue*, Halliday restates the importance of acts of speech.

IT IS HERE, BETWEEN SPEAKER AND HEARER, THAT LANGUAGE IS GENERATED, AND THE SOCIAL CONTEXT ACTUALLY APPEARS WITHIN THE UTTERANCE RATHER THAN EXISTING EXTERNALLY IN A SYSTEM.

For Halliday, children's language development is a process of "learning how to mean". This is not unlike Eco's idea that the adult, who has acquired decoding abilities, possesses an "internal" dictionary (full of words) and an encyclopedia (full of facts) which are actually *one and the same*.

THE CHILD MUST BE CONSIDERED AN ACTIVE PARTICIPANT IN THE PRODUCTION OF A SYSTEM OF MEANING INSTEAD OF THE PASSIVE RECIPIENT OF GRAMMATICAL RULES.

The study of children's acquisition of (and resistance to) language on this basis will therefore tell us a great deal about human expectations of semiotic systems and the motivations behind meaning attribution and creation.

The social semiotic work of **Gunther Kress** (b. 1940) often consists of detailed analysis of young children's responses to and creation of verbal, written and visual texts.

Kress holds that there is a relationship of "motivation" between the signifier (in Saussurean terms) and the sign user.

Many semioticians (e.g. Benveniste) have discussed relations of "motivation" but these have been directed at the concept of "arbitrariness". A motivated sign usually has a close relationship - not an arbitrary one - between signifier and signified, as in the relation of resemblance to be found in Peirce's icon.

What Kress does is different.

Take this drawing executed by a 3-year-old.

For the child, this is a car. Sitting on his father's lap, the child commented as he drew: "Do you want to watch me? . . . Got two wheels. . . and two wheels at the back . . . and two wheels here. . . that's a funny wheel."

Knowing what we do about the vision of a car derived from the average height of a 3-year-old, it is predictable that car = wheels (represented by these circles). Even within the vehicle, the action of the driver is concentrated on a (steering) wheel.

Motivation, then, is a relationship between the sign-user/sign-maker and the means which s/he uses when enacting representation.

From this perspective much can be gained. Studying the whole relationship of signification - why children use specific signifiers to create signs, what their perspective consists of - should enable the researcher to speculate on the way that the adult will construct meaning.

Children may learn at an early age to recognize (and even create) texts in distinct genres of signification. Subsequently, components of these generic texts may be sufficient to trigger expectations on the part of the adult which will determine the way in which they decode communication.

Kress' social semiotic work in literacy and pre-literacy is indisputably crucial in anticipating decoding strategies in the present *and* the future of semiosis.

Semiotic Solutions

For those who can't wait for the future and wish to be semiotic wheeler-dealers in the here and now, look no further than the example of Semiotic Solutions (SS).

Founded in London by Virginia Valentine, SS is a research-based consultancy which assists image makers, corporate planners and product developers in the creation of their strategies.

Using a structuralist semiotic method, influenced by Lévi-Strauss and Greimas, SS demonstrate quite simply to the industry that...

EVERY FORM OF COMMUNICATION (E.G. EVERY AD, EVERY PACK) CARRIES MORE INFORMATIONAL BAGGAGE THAN ANY OF ITS ORIGINATORS REALISE . . . AND THIS EXCESS CONTENT IS **CULTURAL**.

WHAT ABOUT THE INFORMATIONAL BAGGAGE OF THE LETTERS "S.S."?

SS make the structuralist methodology go a long way. In the first few years of operation - in the midst of a recession - the company's turnover underwent more than a fivefold increase.

A recent prize-winning paper by Monty Alexander (SS), Max Burt (Abbot Mead Vickers) and Andrew Collinson (British Telecom) shows how the semiotic methodology is used to root out the unconsidered trifles of contemporary culture and refigure them as the basis of a campaign.

Examining telephone use, Alexander and Co. zoom in on the binary opposition of "Big talk" versus "Small talk". Traditionally, telephone use has been associated with "Big talk" and Telecom advertising strategies have simply mirrored this.

So, "Big talk" has overshadowed its "opposite", as can be seen if one considers the difference:

Big talk is represented as	Small talk is represented as
Important	Unimportant
Male	Female
Metonymic ("rational")	Metaphoric ("poetic")
Serious	Trivial
Official	Popular/carnival
"Correct"	"Incorrect"
Emphatic ("meaningful")	Phatic ("noise")

In qualitative research it was also found that the sign-making of respondents with regard to "Big talk" and "Small talk" - a series of doodles - revealed features of the sociocultural relationship to the signifier that Kress examines.

"Big talk" = geometric forms   "Small talk" = organic curves

"Small talk" had to come out of the shadow of "Big talk"

IT'S GOOD TO TALK

One of the key factors in the reorientation of British Telecom's advertising campaign would therefore need to be an elimination of the gender bias that made telephones the province of male-dominated "Big talk". A playing down of the "irrationality" of "Small talk" and a promotion of its suitability for men would need to be incorporated into the advertising message.

The first in the new campaign of ads, fronted by actor Bob Hoskins, set about this task with considerable success.

What Semiotic Solutions demonstrates quite strongly is that there are many people going about their lives unaware of the fact that they are also immersed in semiosis and sometimes "doing" semiotics.

At the last congress of the International Association for Semiotic Studies, panels took place on gesture, artificial intelligence, theatre, cognitive science, cinema, design, politics, time, music, space, biology, Firstness,painting, advertising, law, the Grateful Dead (!), narrative, aesthetics, religion, architecture, the body, humour, calligraphy, dance, didactics, history, regimes of verisimilitude, marketing, and others.

Here, then, is a broad church.

More tellingly, Umberto Eco recently responded at some length to a request to define the domain of semiotics; some way into his answer it became apparent that he was implying it was **the whole of history**.

Further Reading

The literature of semiotics is big and getting bigger. The following titles correspond to the areas covered in this book and may be used as starting points for further reading.

There are two good general books which bring together different traditions in semiotics: S. Hervey, *Semiotic Perspectives,* London: Allen and Unwin, 1982, and the under-used collection of helpful essays (e.g. Eco on Jakobson), M. Krampen et al eds., *Classics of Semiotics,* New York and London: Plenum Press, 1987. Some landmark writings in semiotics (along with some from sociolinguistics, pragmatics and reception theory) are to be found in P. Cobley ed., *The Communication Theory Reader,* London: Routledge, 1996.

On classical semiotics start with D. S. Clarke, *Principles of Semiotic,* London: Routledge and Kegan Paul, 1987.

Saussure's *Cours* can be found in two translations: *Course in General Linguistics,* trans. W. Baskin, Glasgow: Fontana, 1974, and *Course in General Linguistics,* trans. R. Harris, London: Duckworth, 1983. The works of Peirce are also in two editions: *The Collected Papers of Charles Sanders Peirce,* 8 vols., ed. Charles Hartshorne, Paul Weiss and A. W. Burks, Cambridge, Mass.: Harvard University Press, 1931-58, and *The Writings of Charles S. Peirce: A Chronological Edition,* 30 vols. (projected), ed. C. J. W. Kloesel, Bloomington: Indiana University Press, 1982-. These are hard going; it may be best to start with J. Hoopes ed., *Peirce on Signs: Writings on Semiotic,* Chapel Hill and London: University of North Carolina Press, 1991. A good introduction and dual consideration of Peirce and "structuralism" is J. K. Sheriff, *The Fate of Meaning: Charles Peirce, Structuralism and Literature,* Princeton: Princeton University Press, 1989.

Roland Barthes' *Mythologies,* trans. Annette Lavers, London: Vintage, 1996 is a must, as are the essays in the popular edition entitled *Image-Music-Text,* ed. and trans. Stephen Heath, London: HarperCollins, 1996. If you enjoy these, go on to *S/Z,* trans. Richard Howard, Oxford: Blackwell, 1974. Your studies of Claude Lévi-Strauss, on the other hand, can commence with *Structural Anthropology 1,* trans. Claire Jacobson and Brooke Grundfest Schoepf, Harmondsworth: Penguin, 1977.

In terms of the topic of semiotics, the best place to begin with Jacques Lacan is his "The agency of the letter in the unconscious or reason since Freud" in *Écrits: A Selection,* trans. Alan Sheridan, London: Tavistock, 1977. You can provide yourself with a preliminary context by consulting Darian Leader's *Lacan for Beginners,* Cambridge: Icon, 1995.

Derrida's work (like Lacan's) is renowned for being difficult. However, his early writings are eminently sensible. Try "Semiology and grammatology: interview with Julia Kristeva" in P. Cobley ed., *The Communication Theory Reader*, London: Routledge, 1996 and then go on to *Of Grammatology*, trans. Gayatri C. Spivak, Baltimore and London: Johns Hopkins University Press, 1976.

The key writings of Charles Morris are available in *Foundations of the Theory of Signs*, Chicago: University of Chicago Press, 1938 and *Signification and Significance: A Study of the Relations of Signs and Values*, Cambridge, Mass.: M.I.T. Press, 1964. Before trying these you might wish to check out the essay by Roland Posner, "Charles Morris and the Behavioural Foundations of Semiotics" in *Classics of Semiotics* (see above).

Sebeok should be approached through the collection of his essays entitled *A Sign is Just a Sign*, Bloomington and Indianapolis: Indiana University Press, 1991, and his 1972 book, *Perspectives in Zoosemiotics*, The Hague: Mouton.

D. P. Lucid ed., *Soviet Semiotics: An Anthology*, Baltimore and London: Johns Hopkins University Press, 1988, and H. Baran ed., *Semiotics and Structuralism: Readings from the Soviet Union*, White Plains, N. Y.: International Arts and Sciences Press, 1974, contain key texts by Lotman and others in this tradition. This taster may lead you on to J. Lotman, *Universe of the Mind: A Semiotic Theory of Culture*, trans. A. Shukman, Bloomington: Indiana University Press, 1991.

The *Selected Writings of Roman Jakobson*, The Hague and Berlin: Mouton, 1962-87, run to 8 volumes and are worth looking at simply to get a sense of the breadth of Jakobson's work. More digestible are the two smaller collections of writings spanning his career: *On Language*, ed. L. R. Waugh and M. Monville-Burston, Cambridge, Mass.: Harvard University Press, 1995, and *Language in Literature*, ed. K. Pomorska and S. Rudy, Cambridge, Mass.: Belknap Press, 1987. *The Prague School* are represented in various anthologies of writings, for example P. Steiner ed., *The Prague School: Selected Writings, 1929-1946*, Austin: University of Texas Press, 1982. Available for some time, Mukařovský's *Aesthetic Function, Norm and Value as Social Facts*, trans. M. Suino, Ann Arbor: University of Michigan Slavic Contributions, 1979, is a must.

The best commentaries on the Prague School are T. G. Winner, "Prague structuralism and semiotics: Neglect and resulting fallacies", *Semiotica* 105 (3/4) 1995, pp. 243-276, and F. W. Galan, *Historic Structures: The Prague School Project, 1928-1946,* Austin: University of Texas Press, 1985.

The "popular" Eco and the semiotician overlap: try *A Theory of Semiotics,* Bloomington: Indiana University Press, 1976, the essay collection *Travels in Hyper-reality,* London: Picador, 1986, and the novel *The Name of the Rose,* London: Picador, 1984.

Gunther Kress' most recent work can be found in *Before Writing: Rethinking Paths into Literacy,* London: Routledge, 1996. Monty Alexander, Max Burt and Andrew Collinson, "Big talk, small talk: BT's strategic use of semiotics in planning its current advertising", *Journal of the Market Research Society,* Vol. 37 No. 2 (April, 1995) pp. 91-102, gives a flavour of Semiotic Solutions' work.

Paul Cobley
is Senior Lecturer in Communications at London Guildhall University and the author of *The American Thriller* (Macmillan, forthcoming). *He would like to thank Richard Appignanesi, Litza Jansz, Alison Ronald, Emily Elkington and Shelly the cat for their help and encouragement.*

Litza Jansz
is an illustrator/animator who lectures part-time in Animation and Media Studies. Her previous titles for Icon Books include *Fascism for Beginners* and *The Holocaust for Beginners. She would like to thank Paul Cobley, Zoran Jevtic, Tony Goodman, Howard Ely, Clifford Jansz, Norma, Nat, Mark, Miles Arthur Almo Ellingham and Kenbury for support and inspiration.*